THE FORGOTTEN FAITH

THE FORGOTTEN FAITH

ANCIENT INSIGHTS FOR CONTEMPORARY
BELIEVERS FROM EASTERN CHRISTIANITY

Philip LeMasters

CASCADE *Books* • Eugene, Oregon

THE FORGOTTEN FAITH
Ancient Insights for Contemporary Believers from Eastern Christianity

Copyright © 2014 Philip LeMasters. All rights reserved. Except for brief quotations in critical publications or reviews, no part of this book may be reproduced in any manner without prior written permission from the publisher. Write: Permissions, Wipf and Stock Publishers, 199 W. 8th Ave., Suite 3, Eugene, OR 97401.

Cascade Books
An Imprint of Wipf and Stock Publishers
199 W. 8th Ave., Suite 3
Eugene, OR 97401

www.wipfandstock.com

ISBN 13: 978-1-62032-867-5

Cataloging-in-Publication data:

LeMasters, Philip.

The forgotten faith : Ancient Insights for Contemporary Believers from Eastern Christianity / Philip LeMasters.

xii + 152 p.; 23 cm—Includes bibliographical references.

ISBN 13: 978-1-62032-867-5

1. Spirituality—Orthodox Eastern Church. 2. Orthodox Eastern Church—Doctrine. 3. Orthodox Eastern Church—Converts—United States—Biography. I. Title.

BX320.2 L48 2014

Manufactured in the USA.

To Paige

"Who will find a courageous wife? For such a one is more valuable than precious stones. The heart of her husband trusts in her. . . . For she provides good things for her husband. . . . 'Many daughters acquire riches; many do mighty things, But you excel and surpass all.'"
(Prov 31:10, 11, 28)

CONTENTS

Foreword ix

Preface xi

Introduction: How I Got Here in the First Place 1

1. The Burning Bush: God Is Who He Is 15
2. Salvation, Sex, and Food 38
3. Mary: Don't Be Afraid! 55
4. Football, Liturgical Worship, and Real Life 69
5. Fools, Monks, and Martyrs 92
6. Constantine and the Culture Wars 109

Conclusion: A Final Thought 147

Bibliography 149

FOREWORD

In 1963 Timothy (now Kallistos) Ware published *The Orthodox Church*, which went through many editions and became a classic. Now fifty years later Philip LeMasters's *The Forgotten Faith* has entered the genre of books introducing and explaining Eastern Orthodoxy to non-Orthodox readers. Both Ware at age twenty-four and LeMasters at thirty-six are adult converts to Orthodoxy. Ware grew up Anglican, and LeMasters grew up Southern Baptist but attended an Anglican church for several years. Both became university professors, Ware at Oxford University and LeMasters at McMurry University. Both became ordained ministers, Ware becoming a bishop (now Metropolitan) and LeMasters a priest. For both Ware and LeMasters liturgical worship was important in their conversion, and this led to an emphasis on a eucharistic ecclesiology. Both found attractive the sense of historical tradition, the experience of martyrdom, and the element of mystery in Orthodoxy.

Ware's book is more historical; LeMasters's is more personal, recounting his spiritual journey from Texas Baptist to Eastern Orthodox (Ware has recounted his personal journey to Orthodoxy elsewhere). LeMasters seeks to explain Orthodoxy to twenty-first-century American Christians, as Ware did to mid-twentieth century English readers. Thus LeMasters addresses more contemporary issues.

LeMasters, as did Ware more fully, sets forth the Eastern Christian understanding of the history of the church and its claims to be the "one true church," representing the "original teachings and practice of Christianity" but without judgment on other Christian bodies that lack the fullness seen in Orthodoxy. He writes with the fervor of a convert and the balance of a scholar.

The Forgotten Faith contains a good introduction to basic Christian theology and is helpful for basic Christian spirituality. LeMasters in emphasizing the place of mystery in Christianity reminds his readers of important truths, such as Trinity, *theosis* (becoming partakers of the divine nature; an important word and concept for the author), and communion as forming community. He finds it important that Orthodoxy does not put doctrinal and moral teachings up for a majority vote every few years. This book also deals with aspects of Orthodoxy that are problematic to Protestants—rules for fasting, Mary, icons. Here he offers the usual Orthodox response to criticisms.

The book will be useful for the Orthodox themselves as well as others for its practical advice on daily spiritual disciplines and the cultivation of humility. American Christians need the reminder of Eastern Christians in the Middle East who are usually overlooked in the concern with Israeli and Muslim affairs.

On moral issues Orthodoxy stands in tension with contemporary issues in American life and culture. On abortion, marriage, sexual ethics, and euthanasia it holds to the common historical Christian positions. But on these questions as well as on capital punishment, environmental stewardship, and the danger of greed and consumerism the Orthodox operate from theological commitments, not from a philosophical or political agenda.

This book is both helpful and challenging to those in other communions as well as strengthening for those in Orthodoxy. I commend the book to those who want to know more about Eastern Orthodoxy and for its appeal to many of an evangelical background.

—Everett Ferguson

PREFACE

CHRISTIANITY IN OUR CULTURE is often a mile wide and an inch deep. It provides a bit of inspiration and moral guidance that prop up whatever way of life particular people happen to want. Heaven forbid, however, that Jesus Christ should actually require something of us or challenge our preconceived notions about the good life. This book invites readers to encounter something entirely different, an ancient and mystical faith for which people literally lay down their lives to this day. Eastern Christianity is unknown to many contemporary Americans, but believers of every stripe will benefit from learning about a church much older than the denominational divisions so familiar to them. Instead of diluting the faith in the name of popularity and cultural accommodation, the Orthodox Church maintains the belief and practice handed down by the power of the Holy Spirit in the Body of Christ since the day of Pentecost.

What follows is not academic theology for scholars, but insights about what people today may learn from the ongoing witness of this ancient and always contemporary faith. Though Orthodoxy may seem foreign and peculiar at first glance, its teachings and disciplines continue to transform and bless growing numbers of people like myself who did not really encounter Eastern Christianity until adulthood. My hope is that readers will find a similar benefit in their own lives.

This book draws on lessons learned from people too numerous to count, from my wife, daughters, and parents to my parishioners, students, and colleagues. They are not all named in the text, but I trust that the parties involved will recognize themselves—in a positive light—in the pages that follow. Particular thanks goes to Father John Behr, the Dean of St. Vladimir's Orthodox Theological Seminary, for reading the entire manuscript and providing helpful suggestions for revision. Father David Barr and Dr. Paul Fabrizio also read and commented on portions of it, for which I am most thankful. Dr. Fabrizio, who is Vice President for Academic Affairs at McMurry University, approved a semester's release from teaching duties so that I could complete the manuscript. I appreciate his support and friendship very much. Special recognition and thanks are due to Mrs. Judy Surles, my most capable and longsuffering secretary, for working diligently to format the manuscript according to the publisher's guidelines, surely a tedious task. Of course, any errors and deficiencies in the text are purely my own doing.

INTRODUCTION

HOW I GOT HERE IN THE FIRST PLACE

I HAVE A CONFESSION to make. I have complicated the religious lives of several of my friends and students by introducing them to Eastern Christianity. The numbers are small, but I know Methodists who are asking the Virgin Mary to pray for them and even Baptists and members of the Church of Christ who have developed an appreciation for icons, incense, and making the sign of the cross. Though a few have become members of the Orthodox Church, most have not—at least not yet. They have instead remained in their respective denominations and been pleasantly surprised to learn that Christianity is older than the Roman Catholic vs. Protestant divide. They have also been relieved to find out that believers really do not have to choose up sides according to recently invented labels like fundamentalist, liberal, charismatic, or evangelical. This book is for them and others with a similar openness to seeing what they can gain from encountering the worship, spiritual disciplines, and theology of the Eastern Orthodox Church.

Like most Americans, my friends and students had been unaware of the rich witness of generations of Middle Eastern and Eastern European Christians whose story is rarely even on the map of our western religious culture. No matter where my friends and students presently go to church, their spiritual journeys have been enriched by encountering the little-known beliefs and practices of the Eastern Orthodoxy. I hope that the readers of this book find similar benefits.

There was a time when members of this or that church pretty much kept to themselves, at least in terms of their beliefs and worship. But denominations often do not seem to count for as much these days, as Americans increasingly order their religious lives according to their preferences at the moment without much attention given to where their grandparents worshiped. Church affiliations change with some frequency today, and for many people probably more easily than their allegiance to particular sports teams. Increasing numbers of people appreciate insights from unlikely sources, whether Christian or not, in ways that rarely happened in mainstream American culture until the 1960s. In some ways, my journey from Texas Baptist to Eastern Orthodox fits within this trajectory of restless spiritual seekers finding what works for them on their own terms, or perhaps of religious consumers shopping around until they find what they like. From a different perspective, however, those ways of putting it fail to do justice to a pilgrimage to the Orthodox Church, which I believe to be the fullness of the Body of Christ and which has challenged and changed me and my family in many ways. There is much more at stake here than a customer getting what he wants or an individual looking for someone to tell her what she wants to hear. And as in marriage, parenting, and much else, things rarely turn out exactly as we had anticipated. Of course, that is what makes life interesting and rewarding in surprising ways.

To avoid unnecessary confusion, remember that "Orthodox" does not mean "Jewish." The word itself means both "right worship" and "right belief." So simply put, the Orthodox Christian Church understands itself both to praise and teach about God in accordance with what the Holy Spirit has revealed to Christ's followers ever since the day of Pentecost. The Orthodox Church believes itself to be the original Church in unbroken, living continuity with the faith and practice of the apostles. By becoming a member of the Orthodox Church, I embraced the faith and life of the original body of believers founded by Jesus Christ and passed down across the centuries by generations of righteous people, including martyrs, monks, emperors, peasants, immigrants, and even athletes like Troy Polamalu of the Pittsburgh Steelers. Americans who do not live in major cities or areas where Greeks, Arabs, and Eastern Europeans have immigrated will likely have little knowledge of the Orthodox Church and probably will not know any of its members. So here are a few historical markers to make clear what we mean when we refer to Eastern Orthodox Christianity.

Most everyone knows something about the differences between Protestants and Roman Catholics. Methodists, Baptists, Presbyterians, Lutherans, Episcopalians, etc., have their roots in one way or another in the Protestant Reformation of the sixteenth century in Western Europe, when figures such as Martin Luther and John Calvin protested against abuses in the Roman Catholic Church with a view toward reform. They were especially concerned to reject traditions and practices that were contrary to the

New Testament's basic gospel message of salvation by grace through faith in Jesus Christ. When Rome did not agree to reform itself in accordance with their various teachings, Protestants broke off to start their own churches that reflected the beliefs of the different groups. To put things in historical perspective, there simply were no Protestants before the sixteenth century. *That means that the basic dichotomy that defines Christianity in Western culture did not even exist for the first three quarters of the history of the Church.* Christians were either Roman Catholic or Eastern Orthodox.

Though it is true that some divisions occurred in Christianity during the first thousand years of its existence, the first major separation that significantly impacted the religious experience of Europe occurred in AD 1054 and is known by historians as the Great Schism.[1] By this time, the original Roman Empire in the West was long gone and Christians in Western Europe had come to view the bishop of Rome as the monarch of the Church who had authority to rule over all other bishops and churches around the world. St. Peter had been the first bishop of Rome and the West came to interpret the Lord's statements about Peter's authority as applying exclusively to those who held that office (Matt 16:18–19). Also by this time, popes had endorsed the addition of the phrase "and the Son" (*filioque* in Latin) to the paragraph of the Nicene Creed on the procession of the Holy Spirit. (Do not worry if the significance of that point is as clear as mud; a later chapter will explain it.) In other words, the Western Church had changed the basic statement of faith on its own authority without even consulting the Christians of the East.

The Eastern Church certainly saw things differently. The Church in the Byzantine Empire, Russia, Eastern Europe, and the Middle East had always viewed the bishop of Rome as the most senior bishop of the Christian Church, but not as its spiritual king. He was to preside over meetings with the other bishops, but not to claim authority over them in the regular administration of their churches. On matters that concerned the entire Church, the East followed the ancient practice of bishops working together in councils to discern how the Holy Spirit was leading the Body of Christ. Likewise, the Christians of the East were dismayed that the West had changed the wording of the Nicene Creed. Push came to shove when

1. Ware, *The Orthodox Church*, 311–14, provides an account of the relationship between the Eastern Orthodox Church and both the non-Chalcedonian churches and the Nestorian Church of the East. Though Eastern Christianity surely includes all three communions and "Church of the East" often refers to the Nestorians, I will use these terms to refer to the Eastern Orthodox Church in this book.

a Roman delegation visited Constantinople—the capital of the Byzantine or Eastern Roman empire—in AD 1054 and insisted that the Patriarch of Constantinople, the senior bishop of the East, submit to Roman authority. Mutual excommunications ensued. And when western crusaders sacked Constantinople, and committed terrible atrocities against their fellow Christians in AD 1204 during the fourth Crusade, the Great Schism was sealed.[2]

The world then knew two churches: Roman Catholic and Eastern Orthodox. Orthodox Christians believe that Roman Catholicism broke away from the ancient consensus of faith and the living communion of the Body of Christ. From the perspective of the Christian East, Catholicism left the fullness and unity of the original Church due to its fixation on the authority of the pope and other unwarranted innovations, such as the *filioque*, purgatory, mandatory celibacy for priests, and a greater reliance on rational speculation than on humble acceptance of the mystery of God. These Western trends set the stage for the abuses of the late medieval period that invited the Protestant Reformation. In contrast, the Eastern Church remained true to what had been legitimately passed down in the Body of Christ by the power of the Holy Spirit since Pentecost and the ministry of the apostles. It is not surprising, therefore, that no reformation remotely comparable to the Western upheaval of the sixteenth century has ever occurred in the Orthodox Church.

There are currently at least 250–300 million Orthodox Christians around the world, with the largest populations in traditional homelands such as Russia, Eastern Europe, Greece, and the Middle East. Immigrants to Western Europe, North and South America, and Australia brought their Orthodoxy with them and established churches that have increasingly attracted others in those places to embrace the faith. Yes, I am one of those converts who has joined the over 1 million Orthodox Christians of North America, but it was not a quick or easy journey. Here are the highlights of that story.

Founded in 1898 by Lebanese immigrants, St. Michael Orthodox Church is one of the oldest in America and is in my hometown of Beaumont, Texas. Two of my high school teachers and a few of my classmates were members of St. Michael. My parents taught, worked with, and knew Orthodox Christians in Beaumont for decades. But I was solidly Southern Baptist in my youth and never participated in any of that church's services.

2. See Noll, *Turning Points*, ch. 6, for an account of the Great Schism.

After high school, I enrolled at Baylor University with the intention of becoming a Baptist minister. There I had some exposure to Eastern Christianity during a trip to Israel, Egypt, and Greece, and also learned to read New Testament Greek. I remember that there was a course at Baylor on the Orthodox Church, but I did not take it. I was so impressed with my religion professors there, however, that I later earned graduate degrees at Rice University and Duke University in preparation for teaching Christian theology and ethics at the college level. I recall attending an Orthodox service during graduate school at Rice, but it made no particular impression on me other than that some of the prayers and hymns were in Greek. A professor at Duke assigned us one book by an Orthodox theologian for a seminar on the doctrine of Christ, but again it did not impact me much.

Though my education in ecumenical settings had broadened my horizons theologically and given me an appreciation for other churches, I remained a Baptist until I was almost thirty, attending congregations that rejected the rising tide of fundamentalism in the Southern Baptist Convention at that time. Eventually, however, I came to long for a church with deeper historical roots and a rich liturgical life that also sustained a serious commitment to Christian discipleship. I also got tired of the "moderate vs. fundamentalist" debate among Baptists that encouraged an unhealthy polarization over simplistically defined theological issues.

Having found angry fundamentalists annoying, I was surprised to discover that angry anti-fundamentalists rubbed me the wrong way also. As my wife Paige and I moved around following my teaching career, we left moderate Southern Baptist congregations to worship first with Presbyterians and then Episcopalians. Though we thought originally that we had found a home in the American version of Anglicanism, I wanted more than the theologically vague and generally undemanding version of Christianity we encountered there. While still regularly attending an Episcopal church, I also seriously considered Catholicism and participated for a few years in a network of small groups that sought to recover the early Celtic Christianity of the British Isles. Through this process, I came to realize that my main objections to Roman Catholicism involved its overreaching claims about papal authority and excessive legalism, neither of which is present in the Eastern Church. Likewise, it dawned on me that the early British and Irish Christians were part of the one ancient Church, which included East and West before the Great Schism, and were therefore Orthodox. The signs started pointing in an eastward direction.

We had moved back to Texas in 1995, settling in Abilene, in order to be closer to our families. Paige is a general pediatrician and joined a group practice there, while I became a religion professor at McMurry University, an institution affiliated with the United Methodist Church. Shortly before our move, I had read an article about evangelicals joining the Orthodox Church, but it took a while for me to catch the Eastern Christian bug. I read all the works of Orthodox theology that I could find for a couple of years and had several long talks with the founding priest of Abilene's fledgling Orthodox parish. Though we were both understandably reluctant to leave the Episcopal parish where our young daughters had been baptized and where we had many friends and liked the clergy and the beautiful building, Paige consented to visit the Orthodox Church for a few months. By the end of that time, our family became Orthodox by chrismation, a sacrament parallel to confirmation in the Western churches. That was in the fall of 2000.

The sense of calling to ministry that I had experienced as a teenager had been renewed by that time. Though never the pastor of a church or anything close to a full-time minister, I had been "licensed to preach" in the Baptist church before going to Baylor and then briefly ordained in the network of small groups focused on early Christianity in the British Isles. For a few years, I had occasionally preached and celebrated Communion in McMurry chapel services and had organized a devotional study group on a weeknight. In becoming Orthodox, I also wanted to prepare to serve the Orthodox Church in whatever way I might be of use.

So I began the St. Stephen's Course in Orthodox Theology, a distance-learning program primarily designed to prepare men for the diaconate, a role similar to that of assistant pastor in Protestant churches. A few years of discernment and guidance from two priests and a bishop eventually confirmed a vocation to ordained ministry in the Orthodox Church, and I learned a bit about patience, obedience, and the dangers posed by my own pride in the process. Abilene's St. Luke Mission ("mission" means a very small congregation) could not support a full-time priest and I was ordained to the priesthood in 2006, after two years of service as a deacon, to become the pastor of our community of approximately 35 souls. Teaching and administration at McMurry remain my day job, as the responsibilities of serving a small congregation fall primarily on weekends or special days and seasons of the Church year. Though I dress pretty much like any other professor on weekdays, I am a man in black clerical attire and assorted vestments for services at St. Luke.

While I was definitely the protagonist of our family's journey to Orthodoxy, Paige has embraced the faith with integrity and self-sacrifice, giving her approval not only to our family's conversion, but also to my ordination and sometimes inconvenient schedule of services and other church work. The priest's wife has a special title in the Orthodox Church, translated from the Arabic *khouria* as priestess, the Greek *presvytera* as eldress, or the Russian *matushka* as little mother. When she does not have to see patients on a Sunday morning, Paige is at church, often helping with the chanting, supplying food for coffee hour, and otherwise being a calm, stable, and supportive presence in the parish family. I could not and would not have made this journey without her.

We were both concerned about how our daughters Kate and Annie, respectively aged seven and three at the time of our conversion, would take to Orthodox Christianity. In Abilene, many people pick their churches based on the quality of the children's ministry and youth group, and it was clear that St. Luke's numbers would be quite small for the foreseeable future. There were other children roughly their ages in the parish, however, and they benefited from the attention given to kids in an intergenerational family, which is one way of describing our little church community. We have been intentional about taking them to conferences and camps where they meet other Orthodox youth and have also allowed them to participate in other spiritually healthy groups such as a Christian-themed dance studio and selected youth activities at friends' churches. Both girls, aged nineteen and fifteen at this writing, remain active Orthodox Christians and their social lives have not suffered as a result. One of the benefits of growing up in a small congregation with little programming is that they know that there is more to Church than hanging out with friends or being entertained. They have also developed an appreciation for falafel, hummus, and Arabic dancing, all of which are in short supply in West Texas.

Granted, the spiritual pilgrimage on which I have led my family is in some ways unusual. At the same time, it is not remarkable for an American these days to leave the church of his youth for other communities, especially for someone who studied theology in ecumenical settings and who moved around geographically a few times before settling down. The path from Baptist to Presbyterian to Episcopalian makes sense as a journey from one of the least to the most liturgical of Protestant communions, and I know others who have made similar moves. Some of the same sensibilities that led me to Orthodoxy have led other former Protestants to Roman

Catholicism in search of a historic and liturgically rich church that has not surrendered to the mores of contemporary Western culture. I did not take that direction, however, because on the points of disagreement between Orthodoxy and Catholicism, the East has maintained the original teachings and practices of Christianity. As I joked once to a curious Methodist colleague, "I went all the way to the end of the denominational line and bypassed Rome." It is worth noting that many of the Orthodox priests in America, and a majority in some branches such as our Antiochian Archdiocese, have entered the Church as adults on similar spiritual journeys. In American Orthodoxy today, our family fits right in.

So did I get what I wanted in becoming Orthodox? On the one hand, the answer is yes because the Orthodox Church holds together so much that Western Christianity has separated. Eastern Christianity affirms both faith and works; both liturgical worship and personal faith; both hierarchical ordering and mystical experience; and both specific doctrinal teaching and an appreciation of the mysterious nature of God. Frankly, I am relieved to be in a Church with an ancient faith that does not put basic doctrinal and moral teachings up for a majority vote every few years and that does not change to accommodate every passing fancy of our culture. The dynamics of sixteenth-century Western Europe did not influence Orthodoxy much at all, though they seem to continue to control the dialogue between Catholics and Protestants in unhealthy ways. Some Protestants and Catholics continue to speak of their ongoing divide in terms as uncharitable as those used by Luther and his opponents five hundred years ago. It is more than refreshing to be outside of those interminable debates, as well as those between fundamentalists and liberals whose presuppositions are often shaped as profoundly by different strands of Enlightenment philosophy as by genuine theological commitments.[3]

Rest assured that the Orthodox Church does not, however, cater to my preferences or to those of any particular human being. The beliefs, services, and spiritual disciplines of the Church are passed down from generation to generation. They were formed in times and places very different from our own and the point is for them to change us, not the other way around. So there is a great deal of adjustment required for a convert to become comfortable with a Church that is not the product of modern Western culture. For example, bishops and councils of bishops have tremendous authority in Eastern Christianity. (We often actually stand up and sing when a bishop

---

3. Noll, *The Scandal of the Evangelical Mind*, ch. 4.

enters the room.) Congregations are certainly not autonomous from the larger Church, and not much happens without the blessing or permission of the relevant bishop. Likewise, the parish priest is the spiritual father of his congregation. He has great authority within the parish as one authorized by the bishop to teach, lead, and console the people.

Worship services are lengthy, conducted according to ancient rubrics, and filled with the tones of Byzantine chant, which is a challenge to learn, normally without the accompaniment of musical instruments. Clouds of sweet-smelling incense engulf the worshipers. The Church calls its members to forgive their enemies, give generously to the poor, and fast from the most satisfying foods for at least two days during most weeks of the year. Lent is an especially strict period of fasting with high expectations for personal prayer, participation in services, and setting right whatever has gone wrong in our lives. We prostrate ourselves on the ground at times, make the sign of the cross, kiss icons, and light candles. Becoming Orthodox is not easy and embracing the disciplines of the Church is a process of growth for new members. Those from Protestant backgrounds often find some of these practices to be uncomfortably Catholic, while those from Catholic backgrounds may feel that they have moved back in time to a period before Vatican II modernized their church. Some adjustment is required of everyone.

Despite these challenges, I am deeply glad that our family made this journey and confident that I have reached the end of my ecclesiastical wanderings. It should not be surprising that membership in the fullness of Christ's Body requires something of people and does not operate according to their every whim. This is the Church that produced countless martyrs who died at the hands of the pagan Romans, the Muslims of the Ottoman Empire, and the Communists of the Soviet Union. Their example reminds us that following Jesus Christ is serious business. He required a lot of the original disciples and still expects a lot of anyone who claims to follow him. Orthodoxy calls all Church members to the basic spiritual disciplines of daily prayer and Bible reading, regular fasting, and consistent attendance at worship on Sundays and major feast days. Though our family does not always meet these standards perfectly, we practice them with far greater commitment and frequency than we did before becoming Orthodox. Spiritual disciplines have become part of the rhythm of our lives and given us an organic connection to the faith. Eastern Christianity knows that serving Christ is not a matter of how we feel, but of who we become by sharing more fully in the life and love of the Lord. The time, energy, and focus that we offer God are crucial in becoming more like him. There is no way to grow in holiness without disciplined commitment on our part, which requires actions that manifest what we believe.

If becoming Orthodox is such an important part of our family's Christian life, it is fair to ask how the Eastern Church views other Christians. On the one hand, we believe that Christ founded one Church, and Orthodoxy has abided in the unity of his Body since the day of Pentecost. At the same time, most self-avowed Christian believers are outside the visible boundaries of the Orthodox Church. They are either Roman Catholic or members of various Protestant churches, including non-denominational congregations. I was a Christian before I became Orthodox and the Church certainly does not deny that there are non-Orthodox Christians. We typically do not re-baptize new members from other Christian backgrounds, but chrismate them in a service similar to confirmation in many western churches. When my mother asked me once whether I regretted my religious upbringing as a Baptist, I assured her that I did not. Orthodoxy is the fulfillment of all the good Christian teaching and formation that I received in the denomination of my youth. I honestly do not think that I have rejected anything from my earlier Christian experience, though much has been completed and put in a larger and healthier spiritual context.

Contrary to fears some have expressed to me over the years, Orthodoxy's claims about being the one, holy, catholic, and apostolic Church do not amount to denying the salvation of other Christians. Unlike some evangelical traditions, Eastern Christianity does not boil everything down to salvation as an escape from hellfire. God alone is our judge and he wants all to be saved, though it is possible for human beings to refuse his mercy (1 Tim 2:4). If the parable of the Last Judgment in Matthew 25 is any indication, at least some will find salvation who did not even know that they were serving Jesus Christ. To say that the Orthodox Church is the original Church and the fullness of Christ's Body is not to make a statement about the eternal salvation of anyone in particular. It is, instead, to say something about the Church, especially that the Eastern Church has remained true to the inheritance of faith and life passed down since the time of the apostles by the power of the Holy Spirit. Other Christian communities have added to or subtracted from that original witness. When other bodies and confessions differ from the ancient apostolic faith, Orthodoxy believes that they have lost important dimensions of God's truth. Just how particular Roman

Catholics and Protestants relate to the one Church founded by Christ is not entirely clear.[4]

St. Paul taught that "no one can say 'Jesus is Lord' except by the Holy Spirit" (1 Cor 12:3). Christians of various denominations confess Jesus Christ with their mouths and believe in their hearts in his resurrection. (Rom 10:9). When Orthodox believers see signs of personal holiness and hear important dimensions of Christian truth taught by others, we give thanks for their witness. I have no hesitation calling faithful Protestants and Catholics my brothers and sisters in Christ. Just what God is doing outside the visible boundaries of the Orthodox Church is up to him and beyond our full knowledge. As later chapters will show, Eastern Christians are quite comfortable with mystery. Orthodox representatives participate in the World Council of Churches and other ecumenical bodies toward the end of calling other Christians to the fullness and unity of the original Church. Self-righteous judgment of others is no business of the Orthodox Church or of any human being. Much is required from those who have received much. Given our Church's claims, we are responsible for being faithful to all that we have been given. So instead of pontificating about the spiritual state of others, the genuine Eastern Christian sensibility is to cry "Lord, have mercy!" as we seek to obey him in humility. And when it is possible for us to cooperate with other Christians in feeding the poor, sheltering the homeless, helping pregnant women welcome their unborn children, reconciling enemies, or otherwise showing the Lord's love to those in need, Orthodox believers welcome the opportunity. In that we do it to "the least of these," we do it to him.

One point that any student of Orthodoxy has to face up to is that of ethnicity. Immigrants from Greece, Russia, Eastern Europe, and the Middle East brought Orthodoxy to the New World, and they generally kept their ties to their respective mother countries. So to this day, there are parishes in North America with a strong ethnic feel, sometimes conducting services with as much Greek or Arabic or Romanian as English, if not with a greater reliance on the mother tongue. At the ethnic festivals and even the weekly coffee hours of some parishes in the U.S., visitors may feel that they are in Athens, Beirut, or Bucharest instead of in whatever American city where they happen to find themselves. Though all branches of the Orthodox Church recognize their spiritual unity and share in the Eucharist and other sacraments, in this country there is not yet a united administration to

---

4. Ware, *The Orthodox Church*, 307–11.

connect and oversee the dioceses and parishes. Committees of bishops from the various jurisdictions are working to establish the procedures for administrative union. Until that is achieved, however, the Orthodox of America risk giving the impression of being a disunited group of immigrants from various countries, rather than a Church that fits naturally in our culture and welcomes all people. To be known as the local Greek or Russian or Syrian church gives the impression that those of other backgrounds might do well to worship elsewhere with their own kind.

As a very pale person of Scots-Irish and Scandinavian ancestry, I have no discernible ancestral tie to the Middle East, nor can I say more than a few short phrases in Arabic or Greek. At St. Luke, my generic American (or Texan) identity causes no problems, as we are a mostly convert parish that uses English for all services. Our community is not alone in doing so. But even when I find myself in settings with a strong Greek or Russian or whatever flavor, I feel at home. Not only is hospitality a prized virtue in Orthodox cultures, but the very experience of Eastern Christian prayer and worship transcends ethnic divisions. We follow liturgical patterns that go back to the Jewish temple and synagogue and were Christianized by the apostles. The services of the Church are basically the same around the world, though the language used is the vernacular of those gathered. So even if we do not know a certain psalm in Romanian, we know what is going on and can pray in our hearts. The spiritual reality that Orthodox believers around the world encounter is the same. As a Greek woman told me at a conference in her country a few years ago, "You are just like us!"

St. Luke is an Antiochian Orthodox parish, which means that our spiritual heritage is Arab Christian. The most senior bishop of our branch of Orthodoxy is the known as His Beatitude John X, Patriarch of Antioch and All the East, who resides in Damascus, Syria. His immediate predecessor was Patriarch Ignatius IV, whom I met when I attended an Orthodox theological conference in Syria just a few months before the current revolution began. (Patriarch Ignatius died in late 2012.) St. Luke is Antiochian because its founding members made contact with a parish in Fort Worth that had joined the Antiochian Archidiocese after leaving the Episcopal Church. We have a few members of Arab descent, but are really a "pan-Orthodox" community in the sense of not having a strong or definite sense of ethnic identity. With over half our members becoming Orthodox as adults and English as the language of worship, we would never be mistaken for a gathering of Lebanese or Syrian immigrants at prayer. The Antiochian Archdiocese has many congregations like St. Luke in that respect.

Now that I have provided some context about the Orthodox Church and a bit about my own journey, it is time to conclude the introduction and to get on to more substantive points. The origins of this book are in brief, informal talks that I have given to visiting classes from Abilene Christian University, Hardin-Simmons University, and McMurry University, which have come to St. Luke in order to learn a bit about Eastern Orthodox Christianity. Those institutions are, respectively, Church of Christ, Baptist, and United Methodist, but their students come from a wide variety of religious backgrounds. I have been impressed by the positive response to these talks and the desire of many students, as well as friends and colleagues, to incorporate some dimensions of Orthodox theology and spirituality into their own lives.

This book presents insights from the Eastern Church that Christians of other traditions should be able to appreciate on their own terms. Though many Orthodox practices and beliefs may seem quite far from the experience of Protestants and Catholics, I have attempted to find points of contact to enable any reader to understand why the members of our Church believe, worship, and live as they do. If this book serves to enrich the spiritual lives of those who read it and to encourage them to learn more about Eastern Christianity, it will have met my goal in writing it. Since Orthodoxy appeals to the original consensus of the first thousand years of Christianity, it is not surprising when Christians of any affiliation resonate with it. Eastern Orthodox Christianity has maintained the roots, the common heritage, of all Christians. Any believer who looks at the theology, worship, and spirituality of the Eastern Church will find much that is strangely familiar and appealing.

Since this is more a popular than a scholarly book, I have provided relatively few footnotes. This little volume does not provide a comprehensive introduction to Orthodox Christianity, but instead seeks to reflect a few rays of light from the East that I hope my readers will find interesting and beneficial. And if they complicate your spiritual life, know that you were warned.

I

THE BURNING BUSH

GOD IS WHO HE IS

MY FATHER PASSED AWAY a few days after his ninety-fourth birthday. Daddy was by nature a quiet, reserved person. When I was growing up, people often assumed that he was my grandfather because he had turned fifty the year I was born. I still love, respect, and admire my father and am thankful to have had him as my primary example of how to be a husband and a dad. I could not have asked for a better role model.

Daddy remains, nonetheless, a mystery to me in some ways. Let me be clear: that is not a criticism, but a simple statement of fact. He had already lived half a century before I was born. The Great Depression and World War II were his formative experiences as a young adult, while I grew up in post-Vietnam and post-Watergate America. He was widowed without children before marrying my mother, then my brother and I came along a few years later. A colonel in the Army Reserves and a high school assistant principal, Daddy had a quiet authority and strength about him. He rarely spoke of his military service and was not one to initiate conversations very often. With the exception of Mom, I imagine that most people heard him say very little, at least once he was done making announcements over French High School's public address system. My friends in Beaumont even joked once that he probably communicated with our family by writing messages on a chalkboard. But Daddy was not aloof or disinterested in others. He was simply quiet and did not have to have the first or last word. I wish I were more like him in that respect. The world should have more people like Claude LeMasters.

These memories of Daddy remind me that, no matter how much we love someone, they remain mysteries to us in at least some ways. People are not math problems or chemistry equations. Even if we can often predict what they will say or do, we never know their thoughts, feelings, or motives with perfect clarity. Even if we did, we would likely misinterpret them due to our own issues. Quiet people may seem a bit more mysterious than the rest of us, but even compulsive talkers are beyond our full grasp. We hear what they say, but do not always know why they feel compelled to say it. Even the most truthful statements that we make about ourselves are limited by our vocabulary, self-understanding, and how much of ourselves we want to reveal. The same is true about our knowledge of God. Though many have ignored it, the Bible makes this point clearly.

For example, Moses understandably asked God for his name when he was in the process of reluctantly agreeing to lead the Exodus out of Egypt. It is good at least to know the identity of the deity asking you to garner support for an implausible escape from slavery that could easily result in your death. Moses probably thought "Thanks a lot, God" when the voice from the burning bush said in response, "I AM WHO I AM" (Exod 3:13ff.). In other words, this God is beyond full definition or rational comprehension; to obey him is going to require lots of trust. To know someone's name in that time and place was to have a certain power over them. Magicians were used to saying the magic words and getting the results they wanted. Well, the God of the burning bush is nothing like that. So Moses had to step out in faith to serve a God who remained in many ways a mystery.

If even our parents, spouses, children, and best friends are beyond our full rational comprehension, how much more must that be true with the Almighty? Even our best efforts to name, define, and control him will always fall short. The imagery of the call of Moses makes that point clear. God spoke to him from a burning bush that was not consumed by the flames. Moses had to take off his shoes and then fell on his face before the Lord. This was not a simple exchange of ideas or even a graduate seminar in theology. A mortal human being (who already had a checkered past) truly encountered God, the Creator of heaven and earth, and was told his name. It was not time for conventional chitchat or even sophisticated philosophy. It was time to bow down in worship.

Eastern Orthodox Christianity remembers Moses when it comes to talking about God. We learn from him that true knowledge of God is participatory and relational; ultimately, it is about worship and prayer, not intellectual definitions. The point is not to rest content with mouthing abstract truths or doctrines about the Lord. The goal is to enter into his life and to be transformed by his grace.

If that sounds too mystical, consider this example. An iron poker left in a roaring fire will eventually become red hot. While remaining iron, it takes on heat and light, key qualities of fire. It is transformed by being in the fire. The same will be true of human beings who open their hearts to God in prayer, as they are filled with the gifts of the Holy Spirit and as they show Christ's love to their neighbors. As people find healing from the wounds of sin in their lives and grow as Christians, they share more fully in God's salvation. Our Savior said that his followers are to be perfect as their Father in heaven is perfect, so we all have a long way to go (Matt 5:48). In the Orthodox Church, we call this process *theosis*, which means advancing in holiness and union with the Lord. You might say that we become like an iron left in the Burning Bush (yes, the capital letters are intentional). As St. Peter put it, we become "partakers of the divine nature" by grace (2 Peter 1:4).[1]

Well, what do these fiery images have to do with knowing God? Actually, they get to the heart of the matter. Historic Christianity has doctrines about God as Father, Son, and Holy Spirit, Jesus Christ as divine and human, and other matters that are fundamental to the faith. In case all the talk about mystery has you wondering, the Eastern Orthodox Church does not fudge on doctrine at all. We believe that the Holy Spirit has led the Church across the centuries in defining what needed (and still needs) to be taught in order to proclaim the fullness of salvation in Jesus Christ. But theological claims do not exist for their own sake. Instead, they are necessary to protect and point to the mystery that is beyond words. And even the best words that we use do not plumb the depths of God. We remain mortals who need to take off their shoes and fall on their faces before the Lord. He is God Almighty and we are certainly not.

Consider a concrete example. The Council of Chalcedon made clear in AD 451 that Jesus Christ is one person with two natures.[2] Our Savior is the God-Man, fully divine and fully human at the same time. He does not mix up these natures in a way that makes him neither divine nor human. He

---

1. See Ware, *The Orthodox Way*, 124ff., and *The Orthodox Church*, 231ff., for an account of *theosis*.

2. See Kelly, *Early Christian Doctrines*, especially chs. 9–12, for an introduction to the theological issues at stake from Nicaea to Chalcedon.

is both—full, complete, and unchanged. The Council taught this doctrine because of debates between different theologians who had compromised either the Lord's divinity or his humanity, such that the Church would not be able to give an account of how he is the Savior. If Jesus Christ is not fully God, how can he conquer death and bring us into the eternal life of God? If he is not fully human, how can he save us who are fully human? Very important matters were at stake in Chalcedon.

But a moment's thought will show that these definitions point to a mystery that is beyond definition. Even the technical language used by the council was negative in the sense of ruling out errors more than making positive statements. Surely, no one could ever prove beyond question that the Lord is both fully human and divine—or even explain precisely how the Incarnation works. It would do more harm than good to say that we had. We are speaking here of matters of faith, which, by definition, are beyond full explanation by rational proof.

That does not mean, of course, that they are not true. Think for a moment about the human beings you love the most in this life. You can make statements about them of which you are totally convinced. But you cannot put their generosity, humility, faithfulness, empathy, or beautiful personalities under a microscope. You have to experience them as you do in order to know what you know about them. Your relationship is your knowledge of them; there is nothing objective about it. You also probably do not have full-blown theories to explain your loved ones and their characteristics. People are mysteries, not ideas, and we have to accept that living, breathing human beings are beyond our full rational comprehension.

The words and ideas that we use to describe our loved ones are very important, however. In light of what we have experienced, we do the best we can to express the truth about another person. The same is true for how we talk about God. We use language that is faithful to our experience of the Lord, that witnesses to what we have seen and heard. We have no right to use language about other human beings that distorts their identity or is not true to how we have known and experienced them. Likewise, the Orthodox Church sticks with teachings about God that reflect the experience of many generations of faithful believers. And we are not concerned only with formal dogmatic pronouncements. Hymns, icons, worship services, prayers, and the accounts of the lives of holy people we call saints all point to how God has revealed himself to us. Everything in the life of the Church should protect that precious truth, even if the truth is not terribly popular.

In some more circles today, it is fashionable to avoid using any masculine language for God at all for fear of putting down women. I have also heard of people who did not have a good relationship with their dads and consequently do not like to think of God as Father. Some simply say "God" instead of "Father," while others have invented new trinities such as "Creator, Redeemer, and Sustainer" or even "Lover, Mother, and Friend."

Eastern Christians believe that these developments are misguided and spiritually dangerous. The revealed names for God have to do with mystery and call for prayer and worship, not editorial revision. In the events described in the Old Testament, God revealed Himself as "I AM WHO I AM." The New Testament describes God's self-revelation as Father, Son, and Holy Spirit. When St. John the Baptist baptized Jesus Christ, the voice of the Father proclaimed "This is my beloved Son with whom I am well pleased," while the Holy Spirit descended upon Christ in the form of a dove (Matt 4:16–17). The Holy Trinity is not the speculation or invention of academic theologians, but the truth about God as revealed directly by him. And in case there is any doubt about using the term *Father*, remember how the Lord instructed the disciples to pray, saying "Our Father." Yes, that is the Lord's Prayer from the Lord himself, the incarnate Son of God. It is hard to get better theological support than that.

Of course, language about the Trinity fits the category of mystery.[3] The Council of Nicaea in AD 325 rejected Arius's teaching that Jesus Christ was not fully divine and insisted that the Father and Son are of a common nature or essence. The First Council of Constantinople in AD 381 clarified that the Holy Spirit is also the Lord and giver of life who is worshiped and glorified together with Father and Son. Here is the formal articulation of the doctrine of the Holy Trinity. Precisely how three are one and one is three is surely beyond rational calculation. The math does not add up. Of course, we are not dealing here with counting chickens, but with bowing before the mystery as revealed to us in Jesus Christ and his Body the Church. Christians invoked the Trinity in prayer and baptism from the origins of the faith. God revealed himself as Trinity in the Lord's baptism, and formal definitions of the doctrine became necessary when Arius and others denied that Jesus Christ is really divine. Had there been no controversy about such issues, councils to resolve the disputes would not have been called.

---

3. See Alfeyev, *The Mystery of Faith*, ch. 3, for a discussion of the Trinity in Orthodox theology.

Many people's eyes glaze over when the conversation turns to such seemingly abstract matters. There is nothing theoretical about this debate, however. Questions of the divinity of the Son and the Holy Spirit are crucial for a faith in which people experience Jesus Christ as their Savior and worship him as God. The same is true for the Holy Spirit, as it is by his power that Christ is in our hearts and we find salvation. Just look at how the Lord's followers were transformed on the day of Pentecost and continue to be strengthened to this day by the gifts of the Holy Spirit (Acts 2:1ff.). Ways of speaking about Jesus Christ and the Holy Spirit as less than divine were not true to the experience of the Church and distorted what God had revealed to his people. Had the Church not boldly proclaimed that the Father, the Son, and Holy Spirit are all equally God, the Christian faith would have been mortally wounded. A Jesus who is not divine cannot bring us into the eternal life of God. And without a divine Holy Spirit, how can Christ live in our hearts? (E.g., Gal 4:6.)[4]

Likewise, to reject the use of the term *Father* for reasons having to do with gender or other reservations reflects a failure to appreciate the mystery of God.[5] When Christians call God our Father, we do not mean that he is a little old man in heaven with a white beard. The Father was never incarnate, never became part of his creation with a body, while gender distinctions are bodily and biological. He is in so many ways a mystery to us. The Church actually does not say much about him in the Nicene Creed. "I believe in one God, the Father Almighty, maker of heaven and earth and of all things visible and invisible." Yes, that is it.

We do know that the Father so loved the world that he gave his only begotten Son that all who believed in him should not perish, but have everlasting life (John 3:16). The parable of the Prodigal Son, spoken by the Son of God, portrays a shockingly humble, forgiving, and loving Father who treated his rascal of a son in a way that no self-respecting father of that time and place would have done (Luke 15:11–32). The clues that we get about the character of the Father from Jesus Christ are certainly not those of an oppressive male chauvinist. Christ has truly shown us the Father and we should like what we see.

---

4. See Basil the Great, *On the Holy Spirit*, for a classic expression of the Church's faith in the Holy Spirit.

5. See Belonick, *Feminism in Christianity*, especially ch. 2; and Alfeyev, *The Mystery of Faith*, 20–21.

My father was a great person and I will love and miss him for the rest of my life, but he is not the model for God the Father. It is the other way round. Whatever goodness we find in our own fathers is a dim reflection of a divine love so wonderful that it is beyond our comprehension. And whatever evil or corruption we find in our own fathers, or in ourselves as parents, has nothing to do with the Father, but a lot to do with us. Anyone who uses the Father as a justification to belittle women or abuse anyone is guilty of blasphemy. That is simply not who God the Father is. Whenever I am less than patient, selfless, and generous with my own daughters, I fall short of the true model of fatherhood and need to ask their forgiveness and to repent.

Unfortunately, some Christians today have basically ditched the Trinity to talk about God and Jesus Christ with ever so little mention of the Holy Spirit. I remember a time years ago when my students would sometimes write "God and Jesus love you!" on the sidewalks of our Methodist-related campus. I would tell them that that way of putting it implies that the Savior is not divine and could easily be said, for example, by Muslims and others who view him as merely a great teacher or prophet. (They probably did not appreciate it at the time, but maybe they learned something.) That is precisely the problem with putting aside the language of the Trinity, for it points so clearly to the mystery of our salvation. If we want to proclaim and protect the fullness of the Christian experience of salvation, we need to speak of God as Father, Son, and Holy Spirit.

The Eastern Church stresses that the Holy Trinity is comprised of three Persons who relate to one another in distinct ways. The Father begets the Son, while the Holy Spirit proceeds from the Father. All that we know about the difference between begetting and proceeding is that they are not the same. (Yes, the great teachers of Orthodoxy actually say that!) God is a communion of love in which three persons share a common divine nature in unique ways. The Holy Trinity is the model for marriage, the family, the Church, and all social interactions from friendships to international relations. To be in the divine image and likeness is to respect the uniqueness and difference of persons, even as we love them. We become more fully ourselves as we let others be who they are and grow through the joys and challenges of knowing them.

Eastern Christianity uses the original wording of the Nicene-Constantinopolitan Creed of the fourth century to speak of the relationship of the Holy Spirit to the Father. We believe in "the Holy Spirit, the Lord and Giver of life, who proceeds from the Father, Who with the Father and the Son together is worshiped and glorified." The Roman Catholic Church added "and the Son" (*filioque* in Latin) to that sentence. Catholics, as well as Protestants who use the creed, affirm that the Holy Spirit proceeds from the Father and the Son. This phrase was added to stress Jesus Christ's full divinity against Arians who wanted to downplay the sense in which he is God, as that heretical group did not affirm that the Son is fully divine.

From an Orthodox perspective, the change in wording is unnecessary, misguided, and fails to respect the mystery of God's self-revelation. The section of the creed on Jesus Christ clearly and emphatically affirms that he is of one divine nature or essence with the Father. It was directed against Arius and speaks for itself. Christ himself teaches in John 15:26 that the Holy Spirit proceeds from the Father. He alone is begotten of the Father and the Spirit alone proceeds from the Father, as they have unique relationships of origin with him. Since we are dealing with God's self-revelation as the Holy Trinity, these are matters beyond complete human understanding or definition. The Orthodox sensibility is that it is best to bow before the mystery rather than to fall into rational speculation that does more harm than good.

For example, saying that the Holy Spirit proceeds from the Father and the Son inevitably downplays the dignity of the Holy Spirit, making him in effect the low man on the totem pole. He becomes subordinate to the other two members of the Trinity. Since the Spirit's role is crucial in our experience of participation in the life of God, marginalizing him is no small matter. The true knowledge of God is personal and experiential, not a matter of coldblooded rational analysis. To deemphasize the uniqueness and importance of the Holy Spirit in order to strengthen an argument about the divinity of Christ is self-defeating. They are both God in distinctive ways, and it is better to allow the mystery of their respective roles in our salvation to stand than to build up one by putting down the other.

This change in the creed was also uniquely Western and ultimately endorsed by the Roman papacy in the eleventh century. It was never the faith the entire Church East and West; indeed, its addition violated the very canons of ecumenical creeds which themselves ruled out any future changes or revisions. The *filioque* remains a serious point of contention between Eastern Orthodoxy and Roman Catholicism. The Western use of the term has played an important ongoing role in the separation of the churches.[6]

---

6. See Pelikan, *The Christian Tradition: A History of the Development of Doctrine, Vol.*

The Eastern Church has traditionally placed more emphasis on the uniqueness and interrelationship of the members of the Holy Trinity than has the West, which has often given greater stress to the common divine essence shared by the three persons. Orthodoxy insists that the Father is the personal source of unity for the Trinity. Not an impersonal essence, but the person of the Father is the origin of the Son and the Holy Spirit, each of which has a unique relationship with him. The very nature of God is personal and relational.

Contrary to some of the bad popular theology you may have encountered, God the Father is not a solitary king who dominates everyone and everything in the universe. He works with the Son and Holy Spirit to bring us into their common life by grace. We will always remain human beings, but God calls us to become like that iron in the fire: perfect as the Father is perfect and participants in the divine nature (2 Pet 1:4). Surely, we will become more fully who we are as distinct persons by sharing more fully in the holiness of God, since it is our nature to be in God's image and likeness.

There are parallels in family life. As Claude and Joy's son, Dick's brother, Paige's husband, and Kate and Annie's father, I enjoy an enriching set of family relationships. As a dean and professor at McMurry University and the parish priest of St. Luke Orthodox Church, I am blessed with other relationships that present both joys and challenges. I also have a lot of friends and mostly pleasant acquaintances, two dogs, and at least two cats. Through the struggles and blessings of all these dynamics, I pray that I will continue to grow as a person. In ways that I cannot fully understand, God provides opportunities through them to help me become more like him, to grow in the divine likeness, and thus to become more fully the unique person I was created to be. Our relationships with others are an important part of how we grow in holiness.

And that is also an important part of the reason that the names *Father*, *Son*, and *Holy Spirit* should not be replaced by the products of editorial revision. *Father* and *Son* are relational terms; you cannot have one without the other. The proposed alternatives of *Creator*, *Redeemer*, and *Sustainer*, for example, do not even imply a relationship between three persons. The same is true of *Lover* and *Mother*, which do not necessarily have anything to do with one another, unlike *Father* and *Son*. While *Parent* and *Child* come closer, the uniqueness is lost. No one is so generic as to be merely a parent or a child. We are father or mother, son or daughter.

2, 183ff., for an account of the controversy over the *filioque*.

In addition, terms like *Lover, Creator, Redeemer,* and *Sustainer* point more to actions than to persons. The members of the Holy Trinity work together to love, create, redeem, and sustain the universe and all of us. Their common life is an abiding union of love and holiness. Persons, not actions, participate in such a union, such a relationship. Instead of obscuring these profound dimensions of God's self-revelation because they challenge our preconceived notions, Christians do better to embrace the mystery. Moses did not correct "I AM WHO I AM" or say "Try again it, Lord," and neither should we.

If you are thinking that this approach falls prey to simplistic literalism, think again. The point is not that the definitions of a few words totally explain God or that he is simply the equivalent of what those words normally mean to us in the English (or any other) language. We speak of husbands, wives, children, and friends, but there is a mystery to other people that is not overcome by using those terms. My wife is Paige and my daughters Kate and Annie. Yes, those are their names, but to know and love them as unique and irreplaceable persons is ultimately beyond words. People are not simply the sounds that words make. The same is true for our language about God. The words point beyond themselves to a truth beyond our comprehension. We are back to taking off our shoes and falling on our faces before the Lord of Hosts. It is time for prayer and worship, not for bandying words.

We probably do not go around changing the names of our friends due to our own preferences; if we did, we would not have many friends. Likewise, we have no right to change the name of God. The point is not to make him in our image, but for us to accept that he has made us in his. Of course, we may and should ask questions about what it means to use the traditional language of the Trinity. It is necessary to point out ways in which Father and Son are not identical with the fathers and sons we experience in daily life. The Holy Spirit is different from school spirit, Dickens's "Spirit of Christmas Past," hard liquor, and anything else in creation that goes by a similar name. Indeed, all three members of the Trinity are totally unique, which should not be surprising since no one else is God. Theologians call this approach negative or *apophatic* theology, in the sense of recognizing the limits and brokenness of even the best rational concepts and words about the Lord.[7]

In case all this seems too highfalutin' and sophisticated, let me reminisce a bit about Woodland Baptist Church in Beaumont, the little Texas

---

7. Ware, *The Orthodox Way,* 14–15.

Baptist congregation in which I grew up, where preachers taught that truly knowing the Lord is not the same as knowing about him. It is one thing simply to affirm intellectually that Jesus Christ died and rose again for our salvation, as it would be to acknowledge that George Washington was America's first President. It is another, however, to trust and experience Christ as one's own Savior—to be born again. Though I do not remember Baptist sermons about negative theology, the method is in some ways similar to that of the evangelical preacher. Negative theology helps us realize that words, beliefs, and definitions cannot convey the fullness of God. They are not our salvation. The negative approach refuses to let us worship idols of our own imagination or intellect. It pushes us to seek the true personal relationship and encounter that are at the heart of knowing Jesus Christ and being known by him. That experience of communion with the Lord is ultimately beyond words or rational explanation.[8]

Even the best translation from one language to another loses something. If we stick with one language, different expressions still mean different things to different people. Tones of voice, facial expressions, and a shared history of previous conversations impact what our words mean to another person. We all could tell stories, some amusing and others terrifying, about how we have misunderstood others and they have misunderstood us. If communication is that difficult between mere mortals, imagine how it is when we dare to speak about God. He remains "I AM WHO I AM." All our words fall short.

We still have to speak of him, of course. That is not only how we follow the Lord's command to share our faith, it is also how we grow in understanding. We cannot think without words, ideas, and language, so we want to do the best that we can. The challenge is to remember the limits of even our best attempts. Jesus Christ did not found a philosophical society or debating club. He calls people to believe and obey, to follow his example and commandments, and to participate in his life. To know Christ is to be in relationship with him by faith and repentance. Christians put him on like a garment in baptism (Gal 3:27) and are nourished for eternal life by eating his Body and drinking his Blood in the Eucharist (John 6:53–57). St. Peter said that we are to become "partakers of the divine nature," rather like an iron that takes on the qualities of the fire (2 Pet 1:4).

Just as heating up iron is a process, so is our growth in holiness. It is common to think of Orthodox theology in three stages: purification,

---

8. Lossky, *Orthodox Theology*, 31ff.

illumination, and union or *theosis*.⁹ In the first stage, people turn away from sin and its corrupting effects in their lives. They are purified of the corruptions and pollutions that their misdeeds have brought to them. In the second stage, they open their souls to the light of Christ—they are illumined by him. In the third stage, they reach a union with the Lord that is beyond words or rational description. His holiness becomes characteristic of human beings as they share more fully in his life. The stages are not mutually exclusive, however. Even the saint far advanced in holiness will struggle with temptations and have to deal with the ongoing consequences of sin. The person who stumbles greatly may shine with the light of heaven when he repents. Remember the good thief on the cross whose simple plea to Jesus Christ worked his salvation and the promise of Paradise (Luke 23: 42–43). The progress of our life in God may not be rigidly defined by rational categories. Who are we to tell God the steps he has to take in order to save us?

If mystery remains in the stages of the spiritual life, it should not be surprising that the same is true of prayer. In fact, the highest forms of prayer in the Eastern Church do not even involve words. Truly to pray is to stand in the presence of the Lord with the mind in the heart. That means being fully open to Christ, communing with him from the depths of our being. St. Paul writes that the Holy Spirit teaches us how to pray with groans too deep for words (Rom 8:26). To tell the truth, I am not there yet, not even close. I need words in prayer in order to keep my mind from wandering. That is why the simple words of the Jesus Prayer are so beloved in Orthodoxy: "Lord Jesus Christ, Son of God, have mercy on me a sinner."[10]

Eastern Christians pray them quietly, meditatively, and often. Whenever we are doing something that does not require significant mental concentration, we can silently pray the Jesus Prayer. Someone who is not around anyone else can say the words aloud without causing any problems. As part of one's regular morning or evening prayers, it is possible to devote five or ten or many more minutes to saying the prayer. It is not abstract theology, but a plea that puts us in the proper place before Lord. With this prayer in our hearts, we ask for Christ's help, even as we confess our failings. It is not to be recited as though we are spouting off a formula or impressing God with magic words, but from the heart with full concentration. We are speaking directly to the Lord with the intense humility of the publican who,

---

9. Ware, *The Orthodox Way*, 105–7.
10. See Mathewes-Green, *The Jesus Prayer* and Ware, *The Orthodox Way*, 68ff.

unlike the bold and wordy Pharisee, could only beat his breast and say, "Lord, have mercy on me a sinner" (Luke 18:9–14).

The person praying the Jesus Prayer in this way is a good example of someone growing in the knowledge of God, which means someone who is drawing closer to the Lord. Yes, the person uses words and we believe that the words are true. Though the point is not the particular words themselves, they are necessary for most of us to focus our minds and open our hearts in humility and repentance. If I try to sit in silence for even a few minutes of wordless prayer, my mind wanders terribly. I am no expert at saying the Jesus Prayer, but have found it very helpful to put me in the proper place before the Lord. The more we call upon him with humility and repentance, the more we experience his power and presence in our lives. Our souls become more finely tuned to what he is doing and he responds to our invitation to help us. This is not meditation to relieve stress, but humble prayer to our Savior.

It is unfortunately impossible for human beings to control their thoughts very well. Even our best efforts not to have distracting or unwanted thoughts usually fail. This state of affairs reflects the disintegration of our souls, hearts, and minds as a result of the fall. We are divided this way and that and usually find it more interesting to serve ourselves than God or our neighbors. Evil thoughts and images may well come to us from the outside, from demonic forces that want to lure us away from God. Remember that Satan tempted even Jesus Christ (e.g., Matt 4:1–11). At the very least, the demons can get us so flustered about bad thoughts that we turn our attention from prayer or other virtuous endeavors to obsess about how we could possibly think about murder, adultery, blasphemy, how bad other people are, etc.

So the person who sets out to pray the Jesus Prayer will almost inevitably have lots of distracting ideas. Some of them will grow from the disinclination of our sickened souls to focus on the Lord, while others are darts and arrows thrown at us by invisible enemies who do not want us to pray. The best advice, at least for the beginner, is to pay no attention to such thoughts. The less energy we spend on them, the more we will have for God. In some ways, staying focused on the Jesus Prayer is like staying focused on any mental activity when there is background noise. It is possible to become fixated on the sounds coming from the radio, the traffic, or what others are saying to the point that we are no longer concentrating on what we are supposed to be doing. But everyone knows that it is possible to tune out background noise by focusing single-mindedly on the work before us. That should be our attitude whenever we pray, whether using the Jesus Prayer or other words.

Prayer is mental in the sense of requiring concentration, but it is not primarily an intellectual exercise like doing a mathematics problem. Orthodoxy teaches that we should pray with our mind in our heart, which means being fully present to and open before the Lord. The mind (*nous* in Greek) is the eye or highest part of the soul by which we know God. Nothing should cloud our spiritual vision or distract our focus when we pray from the heart. When people recognize that their minds are wandering in prayer, they should simply turn their attention back to the Lord as best they can. Whether it is an embarrassing memory from years ago, a temptation to commit forgery, or a perfectly reasonable concern as to whether you need to buy more postage stamps, the best thing to do is to give these intrusive ideas as little attention as possible. Do not try to fight them directly, answer the questions they pose, or make them ago away. Just let them be part of the background noise of our lives, the constant buzzing that goes through our brains. People are responsible not for their thoughts, but for how they respond to them. When saying the Jesus Prayer, it is usually best to pay them no mind at all and to get back to more important business.

Before leaving the topic of how to respond to unwanted thoughts, it is important to stress that it is not a sin to have the thought go through our minds to do anything, including terrible acts like committing murder. A spiritually alert person may for whatever reason have such an awful thought come to mind and reject it for what it is, paying the wicked suggestion no mind. Even a spiritually lazy person will consider whether it would really be a good thing to assassinate the owner of the restaurant where he had an overpriced meal, for example, and then reject the idea for the outlandish temptation that it is. But the person enslaved to anger, wrath, and judgment may welcome and nurture such a thought and, if the opportunity presents itself, act upon it. Once someone commits any sin, it is all too easy for it to become habitual or second nature. Orthodoxy calls such sins passions, disordered desires or attachments that we suffer or endure due to the mess we have made of our lives. Obviously, becoming a murderer can put us literally on the road to perdition.

Granted, that is a flamboyant example, but the point is that we should not waste time or energy worrying about whatever unholy thoughts enter our minds when we pray or at other times. As soon as we know what the thought is about, we should turn our attention elsewhere. It is often the case that obsessing about how we could have those bad ideas, what they mean, and how they relate to this, that, or the other thing, will simply wed us to them even more powerfully. Better to simply let them go, say the Jesus Prayer, and trust that God will deliver us. Think of your soul like a person standing by a lake in the summer. You cannot keep flies and mosquitoes from landing on you, but you do not have to welcome them either.

Even better, use repellent. St. Paul urged his readers to focus on what is good, noble, pure, and true (Phil 4:8). When people fill their minds and souls with filth, the results are predictable. For example, watching Internet pornography fuels lust, makes chastity more difficult, and can easily end or at least cause problems for marriages and families. In contrast, when we are fully open to the presence of the Lord, we are blessed and strengthened for a holy life. Despite the struggle to do so with full concentration, saying the Jesus Prayer benefits us because it is an earnest plea from the heart for the mercy of the Lord. God gives some the gift of ceaseless prayer, which in Eastern Christianity may take the form of praying the Jesus Prayer constantly, even in one's sleep. That is not my personal experience, but even a limited use of this prayer of the heart has helped me to grow a bit in paying attention to the Lord and to keep a closer watch on my thoughts and heart. When we turn our attention to God habitually and with all our might, only good can come. St. Silouan, a monk from Mt. Athos in Greece, gave this simple advice: "If you are minded to pray in your heart and are not able, repeat the words of your prayer with your lips and keep your mind on what you are saying . . . In time the Lord will give you interior prayer without distraction, and you will pray with ease."[11]

It is pride, of course, that tempts us to turn our minds from prayer to worrying about how we could possibly have thoughts about sex, food, power, or anything else when we are trying to attend to the Lord. In the moment, it is best just to ignore those thoughts and get back to God. But they may also serve as reminders to be vigilant and mindful, for they help us realize that we are likely to be distracted in prayer and that it is always possible that we will embrace those temptations and fall into sin. Since we are not as holy or strong as we like to think, it is best to keep a close watch on our hearts. Prayer will be a struggle for us until our last breath.

There is a saying in the Orthodox Church that the one who prays is a theologian and a theologian is one who prays. Of course, we do have

---

11. Sakharov, *Saint Silouan the Athonite*, 295.

academic theologians who write books and give lectures. I suppose that I am one of them. But a true theologian in a spiritual sense is one who knows God by personal experience and encounter. To attempt to speak of God without a life of prayer and repentance is very dangerous, for we must be prepared spiritually to think and teach about One who is not a creature of this world. Otherwise, people are likely to make him in their own image and fall into idolatry. The best approach is to let the "I AM" be who he is and know him in the only way he may be known: by prayer, worship, repentance, and a vigilant life of holiness.

Another dimension of Eastern Christianity's perspective on the knowledge of God is the distinction between God's essence and energies.[12] The essence refers to God in himself, as he knows himself from all eternity. Obviously, such mysteries are beyond our grasp. Our knowledge of God is limited to the divine energies, which means God as he has revealed himself to us, especially in Jesus Christ and by the Holy Spirit in the life of the Church. Consider for just a moment how to know something is to master it, to control it. Well, obviously we cannot master or control God. But we can embrace and affirm what God has shown us, from the beauty of the natural world to the blessed life of the Savior.

Our knowledge of God is limited entirely to what he has revealed. What the Lord has shown us is true, but it is certainly not the totality of the divine mystery. That is okay with me, as it is well beyond my present level of spiritual strength to follow perfectly what Christ has already made perfectly clear. I struggle to live up to what I have already got on my plate. Most of us have enough trouble being faithful to what has already been revealed. There is no point in complaining that there are even more mysteries beyond our grasp.

Let's also go further and be brutally honest. None of us has any idea how a virgin could become pregnant with the Son of God as her baby. (A physician once told me that she sees young women who claim that virgin conceptions occur with some regularity, but that is beside the point.) How Christ rose again on the third day and later ascended bodily into heaven is far beyond our understanding. And if we try to give a full account of the Lord's return, the resurrection of the body, and the fulfillment of all things in the coming Kingdom, we will be left speechless—and that is precisely the point. Some things are simply beyond rational knowledge and precise

---

12. Palamas, *The Triads*, 93ff., provides a classic account of the distinction between God's essence and energies.

description. That does not mean that we do not confess them to be true. It does mean, however, that we should not claim greater understanding of them than we actually have. Otherwise, we make our faith and ourselves appear to be quite foolish.

There is a strange compulsion among some Christians to pretend that they know, or at least should know, all things. One of the worst examples concerns the endless speculation about the Lord's return and the end of the world. Christ said that he himself did not know the time of the end of the world (Mark 13:32). When the disciples asked about it, he told them it was none of their business and changed the subject to something more edifying (Acts 1:7). Remember the Lord's parables about always being prepared for his arrival? The servants must be vigilant while the master is away, lest he return when they are unprepared. The householder must be on guard for the unexpected thief in the night (Matt 24:46ff.). The virgins need to have oil for their lamps because they do not know exactly when the bridegroom will appear (Matt 25:1–13). These parables all teach that we have to be ready all the time because we have absolutely no idea when the Lord will return.

How sad, then, that so many waste so much time spinning theories about how world events, American politics, and other passing fancies fit into their fantasies about the end times. The Book of Revelation was the last accepted into the canon in the East precisely because people distorted it in spiritually unhealthy ways. To this day, it is not read publicly in the services of the Orthodox Church for that reason: it is so easily misunderstood. Revelation is apocalyptic literature that places the struggles of the persecuted early Church in the context of hope for the coming kingdom. Eastern Christianity prizes it especially for its accounts of heavenly worship involving angels, saints, martyrs, incense, and beautiful liturgical hymns and practices. It is not a puzzle or a code that anyone is supposed to solve in order to tell us when Christ will return. To abuse the scriptures in this way is to disobey the Lord himself, who made very clear that no one will ever know the answer to that question, at least until the *parousia* itself.

Part of the problem is that Western Christianity has often embraced the rationalism of the Enlightenment uncritically. Please do not get me wrong, our society's affirmation of scientific research, the critical evaluation of truth claims, and skepticism about authority and tradition have produced many positive results. When I take medication, participate in democratic elections, or write with a computer, I am doing what modern Western rationalism has made possible. Problems arise, however, when we assume that the only model for truth is the scientific fact. Water freezes at 32 degrees Fahrenheit, as we know from experiments that can be repeated and verified. In this model, there is one answer to every question and we can prove what that is beyond doubt. Case closed; let's move on to the next issue.

The problem is that God is not a bit of his creation that we can know by objective experimentation and analysis. He is a communion of persons, the Holy Trinity, whom we cannot fully grasp or define intellectually. To know him is to be in relationship with him, to experience and participate in his life. A God who could be put under a microscope or who could be known fully by experimentation would not be much of a God. He would be in our image, not the other way round. It is not popular to say in some circles, but to refuse to bow before the mystery of "I AM WHO I AM" is to show a lack of faith. Like Moses, we are asked to believe in and obey someone who is totally beyond our control, even beyond our understanding. As St. Paul wrote to the Corinthians, Christ's cross is foolishness to the wise of this world (1 Cor 1:18).

To acknowledge that there are parts of the Bible that are likewise beyond our full comprehension is not to a weakness; it is actually a strength. If the scriptures were simply a collection of so many objective facts, we could understand them as well as we do the circumstances under which water freezes. But since the Bible is the written witness to God's saving deeds and message, we should not be surprised that its poetry, sermons, letters, histories, and wisdom literature have to be interpreted as the kinds of writings that they are. They are expressions of faith, true witnesses using the limited means of language and thought in given times and places. The same is true of the Gospels as unique literary portraits of the Good News in Jesus Christ. Try as we might, there are differences among the four Gospels that we do not know how to reconcile fully. If we could accept only that which we fully comprehend as indisputable facts, we would have to abandon the authority of the scriptures or get out scissors like Thomas Jefferson to remove anything supernatural. We would miss the point of the Bible entirely if we did that, however.

If four people provided their memory and interpretation of a dinner party, they would not all use the same words. They would probably get some of the details about what was served when out of order. There might not be unanimity on exactly who said or did exactly what. But it would be absurd to conclude that, due to a few small discrepancies, no dinner party occurred or that their reports were simply made up. And if such variation appears in descriptions of commonplace events, should it be surprising that there are some differences in the details of the presentations of the life of the incarnate Son of God?

For Eastern Christianity, the different ordering of the Lord's temptations in the Gospels of Matthew and Luke, the different genealogies of those gospels, or the variations in the accounts of the resurrection across the four Gospels do not present any real theological problems. The Church recognized the great mystery of our salvation by including four Gospels in the New Testament canon. Had the early fathers been Western rationalists who recognized only scientific facts verified by objective experimentation, they surely would not have been able to tolerate any variations. Then again, that kind of austere rationalism could hardly accept miracles such as the virgin birth and resurrection of Jesus Christ.

Some of my evangelical friends get nervous at this point because they wonder where Christian truth claims find their ground and support if not in a Bible that is made up of so many facts. If the truth of every word in the Bible is not as indisputably true as the point at which water freezes, what is the basis for our faith? To begin to respond to that question, it is helpful to keep in mind that, unlike both Roman Catholics and Protestants, the Orthodox Church does not separate scripture from other dimensions of God's revelation. The Bible is part of the truth passed down in the Body of Christ under the guidance of the Holy Spirit, but not the only authoritative witness to God's truth. The contents of the New Testament were not formally canonized until around the year AD 400, but the Church had been worshiping and proclaiming the gospel ever since the day of Pentecost. The Son of God was incarnate as a human being, not a book. When controversies arose that required clarification on matters crucial to the message of salvation, such as the Holy Trinity or the two natures of Christ, councils met at places such as Nicaea and Chalcedon. They produced creeds and pronouncements that also witnessed authoritatively to the Good News. Councils, creeds, the canon of scripture, icons, liturgy, the lives of the saints, etc., are all sources of theological knowledge in Eastern Christianity. There is no need to choose one and reject the others. The Bible is part, but not all, of the tradition.

The Protestant objection to this approach is usually that scripture is not part of the tradition, but separate from and superior to it. Because the Roman Catholic Church in the Middle Ages developed traditions contrary to scripture, such as works righteousness and the selling of indulgences,

Protestantism has always been suspicious of tradition as merely human invention that obscures the gospel message. The Eastern Christian experience is very different on these matters. Orthodoxy never had or needed a Reformation because the Church did not develop traditions contrary to scripture. The different sources of theological knowledge hold one another in check, for the Holy Spirit works through them all for the edification of the Church. We understand the Bible itself to be part of tradition, part of what has been passed down from generation to generation as a witness to our salvation in Jesus Christ. We want the fullness of that good news and reject nothing that God has given to instruct us in the faith.

Jesus Christ condemned the "tradition of men" that was contrary to God's requirements (Mark 7:6–8). Totally different, however, is the passed-down teaching of the apostles of which St. Paul writes, "Therefore, brethren, stand fast and hold the traditions which you were taught by our word and epistle" (2 Thess 2:15). He even commands the Thessalonians to "withdraw from every brother who walks disorderly and not according to the traditions which he received from us." St. Paul writes well before the formal canonization of the New Testament and shows that the early church was quite comfortable with appealing to teaching passed down in the Body of Christ. And as he wrote to St. Timothy, "the church of the living God is the pillar and ground of the truth" (1 Tim 3:15). There is no reason in Eastern Orthodoxy to play the Bible off against the Church or the tradition.[13]

It is also important to remember that the development of "Bible alone" Christianity in the Protestant Reformation was influenced by the Renaissance. Those seeking the rebirth of western culture wanted to return to the original written sources, to the texts themselves. Our culture esteems the written word and tends to place less confidence in material passed down orally, visually, or by other means that do not produce documents. Enlightenment Christianity also focuses on texts that express moral teachings more suited to rational verification than are accounts of miracles and supernatural events. The point is that there are cultural and historical reasons for how Protestantism views the Bible. Those particular trends were not very influential in Eastern Christianity; hence, it is not surprising that Orthodox sensibilities about these matters are quite different.

And let's face it, things are bit more mysterious when there is not one source of knowledge in black and white about God. If we limit our focus

---

13. Basil the Great, *On The Holy Spirit*, 66, provides a classic statement on the importance of apostolic tradition.

to the written word, even in a book as complicated as the Bible, we will be inclined to think that a good knowledge of Greek and Hebrew, together with a grasp of the relevant historical settings and literary genres, will give us the indisputable answers. There is truth in that approach and Orthodoxy has had its share of excellent biblical interpreters. But the danger in this way of thinking is that God is not limited to the words on a page. Indeed, the same Holy Spirit who inspired the biblical authors also led the Church to include their texts in the New Testament canon. A picture is worth a thousand words, and in the Christian East we say that iconographers write (instead of paint) icons because they are also proclamations of the gospel. The Psalms are the ancient hymnbook of the Church, and the Holy Spirit inspires the ongoing production of music that bears witness to the faith.

If the scriptures are removed from their context in the Church, there is a risk that they will become just another book to be interpreted however those who read them want to interpret them. That is the dominant approach in academic biblical studies in America today and it bears little fruit. The model for finding truth is the individual scholar in his or her office, finding meaning in the Bible however he or she sees fit. That is a great way to make God in our own image, but it is not a truly theological method for interpreting the scriptures as the written witness to Jesus Christ as authenticated through the experience of the Church. Here is another place where we see the influence of the Enlightenment in Western Christianity. The "Bible alone" emphasis meshes with individuals interpreting a book however they want, for there is no other source of truth to norm or regulate a person's reading of the Bible. In Eastern Christianity, biblical interpretation is one of several dimensions of our knowledge of God's truth. The full life of the Church holds interpreters accountable to the common truth that they express in different ways.

As opposed to a deity known only through the black ink on the white pages of a book, it is a bit harder to pin down a God who continues to be known through the lived experience of the Church. In Orthodox Christianity, the full context of the Body of Christ is essential for the faithful interpretation of the scriptures. Every text is read in a context, and even the worst distorters of Christian truth have appealed to the Bible. The gifts of the Holy Spirit have been and continue to be poured out upon the Body (1 Cor 12:7–11). Scripture should be read, interpreted, and applied in light of the dynamic encounter with God that is the Church. The same

Holy Spirit who inspired the biblical authors is at work in the creeds, icons, chants, councils, and saints.

If Eastern Christianity places so much reliance on the experience of the Holy Spirit leading us into all truth in the Church, what is to keep the leaders of the Church from simply making up teachings that serve their interests? The answer would again be the Holy Spirit alive in the Church. For the Church includes all its members, and there have been instances when certain bishops agreed to accept points that changed the doctrinal teaching of the faith. Guess what happened? The rest of the bishops and the people refused to accept those changes. It happened in the mid-fifteenth century at the Council of Florence, when all but one of the Orthodox bishops present agreed to accept papal supremacy, purgatory, and other Roman Catholic teachings in order to get military protection for the Byzantine Empire against Muslim invaders. Bishop Mark of Ephesus alone refused to affirm the council's decrees, but the larger Church agreed with him and repudiated the Council's capitulation to Rome.[14]

In Orthodoxy, the bishops are not so much over the Church as part of the Church. Yes, they have authority to teach and lead, but only the authority given by the Orthodox faith. If they—or any member of the Church—distorts God's truth as experienced and known in the Body, they are corrected by other members. At one level the Orthodox Church is the most conservative Christian community, for it is an article of faith to hold fast to what has been passed down since the day of Pentecost. But the humility of negative theology remains, as it must, in light of the mystery of God. The divine essence of the Holy Trinity remains beyond our grasp, but we cling steadfastly to what God has revealed through his energies, what he has shown us in Jesus Christ and the life of his Church by the power of the Holy Spirit. No, we do not understand any dimension of God's revelation fully, but we affirm that what he has shown us is altogether true, even though it is often impossible to explain beyond question how it is true. Remember the resurrection of Christ, which it is beyond human reason to understand fully. The mystery remains. That is good, because God surely remains "I AM WHO I AM." A God we could define rationally would be someone else.

---

14. Ware, *The Orthodox Church*, 71, reports that "The decrees of the council were never accepted by more than a minute fraction of the Byzantine clergy and people. The Grand Duke Lucas Notaras, echoing the words of the Emperor's sister after [the earlier failed reunion council at] Lyons, remarked, 'I would rather see the Muslim turban in the midst of the city than the Latin mitre.'"

It is impossible to reduce any human being to a set of principles; there is mystery in our relationships with everyone we know. All the more is that the case for God, who is himself a community of three Persons in relationship with one another. He will always be in some ways a mystery to us, but that is okay. We will know him by sharing in his life and becoming like him by grace. It is less like looking for the answer to a math problem and more like becoming an iron left in a fire until it glows red hot. That is how we will know, love, and serve this God who is beyond our control.

2

SALVATION, SEX, AND FOOD

I GREW UP A Southern Baptist, have taught for years now at a United Methodist-related university, and joined the Eastern Orthodox Church in 2000. My impression is that every denomination takes pride in its covered dish suppers, coffee hours, and fellowship meals. They all say, "We Baptists or Methodists or Orthodox or Lutherans or whatever really like to eat." Unfortunately, the pastors of just about all denominations have a well-deserved reputation for being a bit paunchy, as do many of the church members. That is not universal, of course, but overindulgence in the pleasures of the table is all too common in the Christian community. While pastors in the more conservative churches still preach about the dangers of sexual sin, very rarely does anyone speak against gluttony. We like to give ourselves a pass on that one and usually do not take it seriously as a temptation. It is one sensual indulgence to which Christians usually turn a blind eye.

Of course, eating too much does not put us at risk only for spiritual problems. Too many people are fat, really fat, in the USA. Junk food, fast food, too much food—they are all around us. Modern conveniences and transportation have cut our rates of physical activity drastically over the last generation. Despite the existence of so many gyms, hardly anyone gets enough exercise. Obesity is an epidemic and only getting worse, which is bad for our bodies and our souls. When my wife Paige trained as a pediatrician, kids never had type-2 diabetes. Now it is all too common.

We have probably blotted it out of our memory, but the Bible tells us that sin came into the world together with the abuse of food. Everything changed when Adam and Eve could not control their appetites. They ate the fruit of the vine in violation of God's command, and we are still following their bad example. Food is good stuff; there is nothing evil about it at all. The problem is that we use it for purposes other than those for which God created it. We consume food and drink in ways that are not good for us as God's children. Truth be told, we all have a problem controlling our stomachs and taste buds in one way or another. No wonder all-you-can-eat is so popular. And portion sizes at restaurants are so huge that an individual's serving could often sustain a small family. That is sadly ironic in a world where so many in developing nations still starve to death or are malnourished.

Obviously, we need nourishment in order to live. God gives us fruits, vegetables, meat, grains, etc., in order to keep us alive so that we may grow closer to him and to one another. But that is not the only reason because food is also about relationships. Grandmother's brownies and Mimi's chocolate cake—not to mention many other tasty dishes they have enjoyed since early childhood—have a deep and special appeal to our daughters Kate and Annie. I always eat more when I visit my mom's house, for reasons I cannot quite explain. When you invite someone to your home for dinner, you deepen your friendship with them. And who really likes to eat alone? Great food screams for great company, and there is a reason we put out a big spread for Christmas, Easter, and Thanksgiving, as well as special cakes for birthdays and candle-light dinners for anniversaries. Eating together brings people closer together. Remember the line from the old TV ad, "Nothin' says lovin' like somethin' from the oven."

The same is true about our relationship with God. All Christian churches have some form of communion, whether they call it the Lord's Supper, the Mass, or the Holy Eucharist. We remember and are nourished by Jesus Christ's death and resurrection when we gather to eat his Body and drink his Blood. Different groups of believers interpret the meaning of the services differently, but Eastern Christianity is happy to bow before the mystery. In ways that no human brain can define, a miracle happens as bread and wine become by the power of the Holy Spirit the Body and Blood of the Lord. Our Savior said that "whoever eats My flesh and drinks My blood has eternal life, and I will raise him up at the last day" (John 6:54). If that seems strange, just imagine how the disciples felt when they heard these words from a living human being. Many of them gave up following Jesus after this hard teaching.

Well, we know now that the Lord did not mean that people should take a bite out of his arm and lick up what spurted out. Instead, the central worship service of the Church—celebrated every Sunday of the year in

Orthodox churches and many other times on weekdays also—fulfills the original purpose that God intended for food. It gives us life and strengthens our relationship with God and one another. We commune with the Lord and all the other members of the Church when we receive Communion.

The contrast should be clear. Death, decay, and divorce came into the world after Adam and Eve chose satisfying their appetites over God. Instead of advancing in a life of holiness and living in harmony with one another and the world of nature, they acted on their self-centered desires to gobble up the goodies of creation simply because they wanted to do so. And the consequences of their behavior are clear: broken relationships between men and women, struggles with the natural environment, and death (Gen 3:14–24).

Think for a moment about how you feel when you are really hungry. All you think about is satisfying your craving for food. And sometimes we have cravings for food when we are not even hungry. Maybe we are angry, feeling sorry for ourselves, sexually frustrated, or just plain bored. I once ate half a cake because I was upset about having car trouble. In those moments, life becomes about satisfying irrational desires for pizza, ice cream, chicken wings, potato chips, or whatever else we can stuff into our mouths just for the sheer pleasure of the experience. And if you are like me, being very hungry can also make you into a real jerk who is not much fun to be around. Just ask Paige.

Not a very pretty picture, is it? We are created to become "partakers of the divine nature," to share in the eternal life of the Holy Trinity, and to radiate the holiness of God (2 Pet 1:4). Too often, we are more like pigs gorging themselves on slop. The problem is that we simply worship our bellies, taste buds, and the seemingly innocent pleasures of the table. But we do not realize that abusing food—and ourselves—is really the way of death. And I do not mean simply clogged arteries, high cholesterol, and so much weight that our joints and internal organs give out. To be a glutton, to make satisfying lust for food a settled habit in our lives, is to follow Adam and Eve out of Paradise and into our sad world of decay and corruption where we put the false god of self before our true Lord and our neighbors. If we follow their way, then at the end of the day, we will not seek communion with God or other people; we will not care about eternal life either. We will just want to pig out, have sex with whomever we please, get rich, and have our own way all the time. Eat, drink, and be merry, for tomorrow ye die. Sorry to tell you, but that is all too often life in the world as we know it. We are all at risk of taking this wide and easy route to destruction.

Thankfully, Jesus Christ is the second Adam who came to put right all that the first Adam got wrong (1 Cor 15:45). Yes, he ate, drank, and supplied really good wine for at least one wedding party. In fact, he often spoke of wedding feasts as symbols of the Kingdom of God. On the last night of his life on earth, he identified the bread and wine of a Passover meal with his Body and Blood. That is because he is the Lamb of God who takes away the sins of the world. He entered fully into the misery and pain of life in our darkened, distorted world, even to the point of dying on a cross, being buried in tomb, and descending to Hades. He did all that in order to conquer death by his resurrection, to restore Adam and Eve—and the rest of humanity—to Paradise.

Holy Communion nourishes us for the eternal life of the Kingdom. Jesus Christ's sacrifice and victory become present to us when a humble menu of bread and wine becomes resurrection food, the Body and Blood of the Son of God who conquered even the black night of the tomb. It is a wedding feast and we are the bride of Christ, the Church for which the Lamb gave his life. We eat and drink in the Kingdom of God; this meal makes us participants in the age to come. Our communion with God and one another is restored. Yes, Adam and Eve really are back in Paradise. And the original purpose of food is fulfilled, for we are truly given life and brought into communion with the Lord and one another.

The Eucharist is not a magic act, however, because there is a lot in all of us that does not really want to be in communion with God. We have spent a lifetime—and humanity has spent countless generations—being addicted to our own will and pleasure. Old habits are hard to break and festering wounds heal slowly. So unfortunately we are inclined to try to combine the heavenly banquet with a life of self-centeredness that shows itself in how we mistreat others and abuse money, sex, power, food, drink, and natural resources. That is a bad combination that makes us slaves to our desires and tempts us to think that the Christian life is lived only on Sunday morning during a church service. No, what we do on Sunday is not all there is to Christianity. The Eucharist is, however, the meal that strengthens us for a faithful life every day of the week. It is the model for how we should live all the time, offering our lives to the Father in union with the Son by the power of the Holy Spirit. We then go into the world to live out the love and holiness of God in relation to everyone and everything we encounter. We should live as we worship, making our entire life an ongoing offering of thanksgiving to the Lord.

That is the goal, but let's be honest. None of us does it perfectly; most of us do not do it well at all. Some do not even try. We need help in order to have the power to live faithfully and resist those familiar temptations. We are like someone who is recovering from an accident or surgery and requires serious therapy for rehabilitation. I have a herniated disk, and my chiropractor and massage therapist have poked, prodded, and punched me in painful ways on more than one occasion. That is not fun, but they have restored me to something resembling health. Painful therapies are sometimes absolutely necessary if we want to get well. And here is where ascetical fasting comes in. Despite the struggle and inconvenience, we need to deny ourselves, take up our crosses, and push away from the table.

In Eastern Christianity, fasting is a discipline to help us learn to say no to self-centered desires that we have trouble controlling. We call those desires "passions" because we suffer them. At times they virtually overpower us; they control us. Of course, things should be the other way round; we should control them. But ever since that couple in the Garden of Eden put their own longings before their relationship with God, we have been pulled this way and that by out-of-control desires for pleasure. For example, food and the male-female distinction are fundamentally good dimensions of God's creation. The problem is that we have messed up relationships with them. If we are honest, we can all attest to that in our own lives.

Orthodox believers fast by saying "no thank you" at times to the richest, most satisfying foods. I am a Texan, but during strict fasting periods even the Orthodox of the Lone Star State do their best not to consume meat, dairy products, fish with a backbone, olive oil, or wine. So pass the shellfish, fruits, grains, nuts, and vegetables. As Annie once said at the beginning of a fasting season, "Here comes the weird food." We fast on almost all Wednesdays and Fridays of the year, in remembrance of the Lord's betrayal and crucifixion. Fasting during Lent and Holy Week is especially rigorous, as we are doing our best then to turn from sin and toward the Lord as we prepare to journey with him to the horror of the cross and the joy of the empty tomb. The Advent fast covers the forty days before Christmas; it is not as strict and focuses more on joyful preparation to welcome the Savior at his birth. The Apostles Fast (ending on the day in late June when the church remembers Sts. Peter and Paul) and the Dormition Fast (recalling the end of the Virgin Mary's life) occur in the summer and are relatively brief.

If those guidelines for what not to eat seem bizarre, remember that Christianity developed in the ancient Mediterranean world. As in the Old

Testament, wine and oil represented God's blessing, mercy, and abundance. You simply could not have a proper wedding feast without wine, as the Lord's mother reminded him before his first miracle in St. John's Gospel. Meat was rare and expensive; the vast majority of people did not have animals to kill whenever they were hungry. In the parable of the prodigal son, it was a really big deal to kill the fatted calf. (In contemporary America, we would just go to the supermarket, get lamb chops, and think nothing of it.) Even dairy products were often a luxury in that time and place. A poor person without livestock was out of luck. So to follow a diet of fruits, grains, vegetables, and whatever shellfish you could find along the shore was to eat common, cheap, and readily available staples. It was also to reduce greatly the amount of fat in one's diet and to eat nothing rare, expensive, or fit for a celebration. It was a menu of humble food.

This type of fasting also harkens back to the vegetarian diet of the Garden of Eden. It is not until after the great flood that Noah received permission to kill animals and eat their flesh (Gen 1:29–30; 9:3). By returning to a virtually vegan diet, Orthodox fasters participate in a very limited way in the harmony with the natural world that was part of God's original intention for his creation. When we consider the environmental and ethical problems associated with how slaughterhouses and poultry farms operate, for example, the benefits of a fasting diet for all the Lord's creatures becomes evident. To eat low on the food chain is a sign of the peace of the Kingdom for the entire creation.

Of course, hardly anyone is any good at fasting, which is part of the point. We learn humility when we realize how weak we are before barbecued ribs, roasted chicken, and pound cake. Our stomachs and taste buds are spoiled rotten and do not like it when they do not get their way. Fast from steak and it is easy to think of nothing but steak. Yes, we really are wimps. Our desires and appetites are out of control, as anyone knows who has struggled to lose weight or said, "Well, I'll just have one potato chip" before marveling a few minutes later at any empty bag. We are much weaker than we like to think. No wonder it is so hard for so many to lose weight.

Fasting also gives us some training in how to resist bodily desires for pleasure that can overwhelm us and seem impossible to resist. Obviously, it is a great tool for fighting gluttony. Though it is still possible, we are not as likely to overdo it with tofu, garbanzo beans, and broccoli. Learning that we really can live on a modest and healthy menu that does not include our favorite foods is quite a blessing. Yes, life does go on even when we do not get our way and do not satisfy every self-centered desire. Though we eat lots of rich and wonderful dishes at Easter, the rigors of Lent help to heal our lust for food and other forms of self-gratification at least a bit. And having two fast days a week plus four fasting seasons a year provides lots of needed practice. Self-denial becomes part of the rhythm of our life, which is something that most of us need.

Fasting also makes it possible to feast, to enjoy a really great meal as a sign of joy. When you have fasted strictly throughout Lent, you can really celebrate at Easter when you eat the fatted calf and pig and cow. Those who did not fast will still enjoy the meal, but there is an intensity of celebration when you taste meat for the first time in several weeks. Let's face it. We are human beings who naturally like some foods more than others. It makes sense to associate the high points of the Christian year, especially Easter and Christmas, with great meals that bring everyone together in joyful celebration of the Good News. Forty days—or more—of fasting helps us prepare to embrace the blessing of the feast as fully as possible. No, that does not mean gluttony or other sins; it does mean that we will be more appreciative of rich food and good fellowship as signs of our salvation.

Fasting really does help us appreciate food as a blessing. For example, I never gave a moment's thought to olive oil until becoming Orthodox and fasting from it during the strictest periods. Now I have discovered that I miss olive oil when I abstain from it. It really does improve the flavor of other foods. To be especially grateful to have olive oil, fish, cheese, meat, etc., is spiritually healthy because so often—especially in affluent countries like the USA—we take God's blessings for granted. If you want to develop the spirit of thankfulness to the Lord for the splendor of food, do some fasting.

It also helps to be willing to learn to cook and appreciate foods from other cultures that are not based on meat. Thai, Chinese, Indian, and Middle Eastern cuisines include many dishes without animal products that are inexpensive and not difficult to prepare. And with all the cookbooks available today, it is easy to find tasty vegan recipes that are ready in no time. Simply to remove meat and dairy products from the typical American diet is quite a challenge, as that does not leave much that is substantial and satisfying. A bit of experimentation with new recipes is very helpful as people begin to fast, at least in the Orthodox way.

Fasting is not fundamentally about food, but about healing our addiction to self-centered desire. To be blunt about it, we do not lust only for food. When we hear the word "lust," we probably think of sex. Yes, that is because most people struggle with unruly sexual desires of one kind or another. At times, many human beings feel as though they will die if they do not find a way to gratify those urges. Even in faithful marriages, husbands and wives may have unhealthy attachments to sex that make physical pleasure more important than loving the spouse or even God. Since traditional Christianity teaches that people who are not married should not be having sex at all, singles face especially difficult challenges.[1] Pastors, Sunday school teachers, youth workers, and lay leaders need to do more than simply tell people that they should save sex for marriage. They need to help teenagers, thirty-something singles, divorced and widowed folks, and everyone else develop the spiritual and personal strength to respond to their sexual desires in healthy and holy ways. As everyone with any experience of life knows, that is often quite a challenge.

Fasting is actually a powerful tool for growing in the ability to channel our longing for sexual intimacy. Consider for a moment how our lusts for food and for sexual pleasure are similar. They are both bodily urges that have a lot to do with self-centered enjoyment. As we experience them in our fallen state, they are both corruptions of blessings from God that were intended to give life and bring us closer to the Lord and to others. Though it is not entirely clear what it meant in paradise, Adam and Eve were told to be fruitful and multiply; man clings to his wife and they become one flesh (Gen 2:24). We are made male and female in God's image; husband and wife bring new life into the world through their love for one another. The Lord blessed marriage when he turned water into wine at the wedding in Cana of Galilee (John 2:1–11). In the Eucharist, we eat and drink our salvation; the original intended purpose of food is fulfilled as bread and wine become the menu of the heavenly banquet. Christian marriage restores the shattered union of man and woman as a sign of our salvation. The Savior still turns water into wine as the troubled man-woman relationship becomes an icon of the relationship between Christ and the Church (Eph 5:31ff.).[2] Food and sex should ultimately direct us to the Kingdom of God.

Unfortunately, that is not how we usually experience them. Adam and Eve placed satisfying their appetites before growing in relationship with God. And like them, we have wanted to grab all the gusto we can ever since. No one forces us to give into our out-of-control desires, but it is so much

---

1. Winner, *Real Sex*, 123ff.
2. LeMasters, *Toward a Eucharistic Vision of Church, Family, Marriage, and Sex*, ch. 5.

easier to do so than to control ourselves. The need for nourishment and our positive inclination toward the opposite sex are not at all sinful in and of themselves. God created them in order to help us become more like him in holiness and love. We are made male and female in God's image; he placed only one limitation on the diet of the first couple in paradise. But that little bit of fasting from the forbidden fruit was beyond what Adam and Eve wanted to do. Like Johnny Cash, we too have fallen into a burning ring of fire. Our passions often burn red hot and get the better of us.

Instead of drawing us closer to the Lord and to one another, humanity's originally healthy desires for intimacy have become sick, warped, and obsessive. God wants us to channel and control this powerful instinct as we become one with a spouse, together give life to children, and die to our self-centeredness every step of the way. The horrors of rape, abuse, infidelity, promiscuity, and broken hearts occur as the result of our failure to lead holy lives in the bedroom. People become addicted to sexual desires gone wild, seemingly unable to control themselves as all hell breaks loose in the most intimate dimensions of our lives. These matters are personal, but they are not private. At the very least, they impact our sexual partners and the children conceived. They also shape us as people who tend to prize our pleasure above all else. The challenges for a society full of people formed in this way are profound.

The Bible certainly is not shy about these matters. The Old Testament contains racy and embarrassing stories in which great saints such as King David act like someone in a bad country song. He sees a beautiful woman bathing, gets her pregnant, and then kills her husband in order to hide his foul deed (2 Sam 11). Jesus Christ saved the life of a woman caught in adultery (John 8:1–11). He treated a Samaritan woman with a colorful past with compassion and respect (John 4), and defined adultery in a way that gives no one a basis for self-righteousness (Matt 5:28). St. Paul addressed just about every form of immorality imaginable in his letters to the Corinthians, even a man who had shacked up with his stepmother and Christians who thought nothing of having relations with prostitutes (1 Cor 5–6). We often do not have to look very deeply into our own hearts or our own relationships—past and present—for ample evidence that we find it all too easy not to direct our sexual desires in holy ways. And if the point is still not clear, just go to a movie, get on the Internet, watch the news, or listen to contemporary music. When I tell students that my favorite examples of such problems come from George Jones and Johnny Cash, they smile patiently (probably as they would for their grandfather) and tell me that classic country is nothing compared to the realism of rap. Our culture is up to its neck in corruption of the relationship between man and woman. We all suffer as a result.

It is certainly not magic, but a little discipline with our taste buds and stomachs tends to throw cold water on the fires of sexual lust. No, it is not instantaneous; but when we get in the habit of saying "no thanks" to deep-seated physical desires for pleasure, positive changes start to happen. The inflamed passion cools down just a little bit. We learn how it feels to tolerate unsatisfied hunger, which has something in common with an unsatisfied desire for sex. We also learn that not getting what we want is not going to kill us. Yes, we can live through it. Even the deprivations of Lent will come to an end, though it surely does not feel that way a couple of weeks into the season.

It is a sad thing that fasting in a disciplined, sustained way is so rare in contemporary Christianity. No wonder the private lives of Christians often are not much different from those of nonbelievers. Seriously, if we cannot even overcome a desire for a hamburger, how can we hope to conquer unholy longings for sex with someone to whom we are not married? Americans are bombarded by Internet pornography, lewd magazine covers in grocery store checkout lines, smutty news reports that grab our attention by appealing to prurient interest, and vulgar entertainment that would have been rated X a few decades ago. So many unmarried couples live together, while more simply have casual sex; out-of-wedlock births continue to climb; sexual deviancy of various kinds has become commonplace. Abortion is simply part of this way of life. Mainstream American culture approaches sexual ethics in terms of protecting the rights of consenting adults with a nod to public health. So other than condemning rape and the transmission of disease, our society is not of much help in forming people who can direct their desires in holy ways.

Yes, we need all the help we can get in this area. If we are in the habit of eating whatever we want whenever we want it, we are more likely to become slaves to gratifying other bodily desires. The Eastern Fathers say that gluttony is the mother of adultery. There is a lot of truth in that statement, especially in a society with epidemic rates both of obesity and of sex between people who are not married to one another. Overfed and under-disciplined Christians will find it hard to respond to their deep longings for intimacy in a fashion pleasing to God. Fasting is a good tool for fighting many kinds of lust. One good habit leads to another and fasting from our favorite foods really hits us where we live.

We have to be careful, however, because it is possible to fast in ways that do us more harm than good. The Pharisees seem to have done precisely that. If we are self-righteous when we fast, judging others as being worse than we are because of what they eat, we will have missed the point entirely. Better not to fast than to do it in a way that strengthens pride, that most dangerous of passions. In order to be spiritually beneficial, fasting must also be joined with prayer. The Lord said that we live not by bread alone, but by every word that proceeds from the mouth of God (Matt 4:4). If we have not made listening for God in prayer a settled habit in our lives, we will not be able to fast in a spiritually healthy way. We will simply lack the strength to do so.

If someone is important to us, we find a way to spend time with that person, to get to know them better and to enjoy their company. That is why the Orthodox Church calls its members to devote time and energy to prayer at least once a day, ideally in an "icon corner" or another area of one's home set aside for devotions. If something is important to us, we give it space. For example, houses have special rooms for sleeping, eating, cooking, and visiting with others. Likewise, we set aside a place for prayer because this practice is essential not only for fasting, but for the entire Christian life.[3]

Someone who is just beginning to fast has to be realistic. A couch potato who tries to run a marathon may not live to see tomorrow; if he survives, he may well never exercise again. Someone who has worshiped at the altar of the all-you-can-eat buffet his entire life probably will not be able to fast strictly in the blink of an eye. The spiritual fathers and mothers of the Eastern Orthodox Church apply its disciplines pastorally to particular people for their growth in Christ. A physical therapist modifies the standard regimen according to the health and abilities of the patient. It makes sense to be tougher with the professional athlete than with someone who never had much physical strength to begin with. The same approach applies to fasting. We should do what we can do for the healing of our souls, given where we are at this point in our journey.

Leave aside the Orthodox fasting guidelines for a moment, especially if you have no previous experience with this discipline. The person who has never fasted before might begin with eliminating sugary beverages, dessert,

---

3. Coniaris, *Making God Real in the Orthodox Home*, contains many helpful suggestions for prayer, fasting, and other spiritual disciplines in the home.

snacks, second helpings, or huge portions of food. For some, having only one piece of pie—as opposed to two or three—after dinner is actually a sacrifice. We all have to start somewhere. Any discipline, no matter how small, that actually helps us control self-centered desires for pleasure is a step in the right direction. Some people, such as pregnant women and diabetics, should not fast from food. The point is not to make ourselves sick or too weak to do our daily work. It is to humble ourselves with the recognition that our life is in God, not in satisfying every desire that comes down the pike. So if we are physically able to fast from rich food for reasonable amounts of time, we should prayerfully consider doing so. And when our current level of culinary restraint becomes really easy, it is time to take it up a notch. We may never become vegans who eat like birds, but periodic seasons of self-restraint will be of great benefit for most of us.

Though the fasting guidelines of the Orthodox Church are clear, people are at different places in their ability to embrace them. Some simply do not want to fast, and obviously no one can or should make them do so. Others fast only from meat, especially women who need the calcium from dairy products for the strength of their bones. It is often not practical for soldiers and others who are engaged in very physically demanding work to limit their nutrition so drastically. Frail senior citizens, nursing mothers, and infants obviously should not fast due to health concerns. And in a religiously mixed household, the cook should not have to prepare two meals so that one person may follow the letter of the law. The point is the salvation of souls, not inconveniencing others.

A good rule of thumb is to stretch ourselves a bit, but not beyond what we can do with some regularity and without being total jerks to those around us. No matter how pious we may feel, it is not part of Christian discipleship to make other people suffer for our sins. The Lord's advice on how to fast is the best: "Anoint your head and wash your face so that you do not appear to men to be fasting . . . " (Matt 6:17–18). If we cannot look and act like all is well, we are biting off more than we can chew. Better to eat a steak on Good Friday than to devour your neighbor for whom Christ died. As Archimandrite Meletios Webber writes, "And if you are going to say something nasty about someone . . . , you might as well be chewing on a pork chop at the same time."[4]

Likewise, fasting guidelines are not kosher laws. No food or drink is unclean. As St. Paul taught, "Every creature of God is good, and nothing

---

4. Webber, *Bread and Water, Wine and Oil*, 76.

is to be refused if it is received with thanksgiving; for it is sanctified by the word of God and prayer" (1 Tim 4:4–5). In and of itself, our diet is spiritually irrelevant, for "food does not commend us to God; for neither if we eat are we the better, nor if we do not eat are we the worse" (1 Cor 8:8). If eating meat from animals sacrificed to idols could make St. Paul's brother stumble, the challenge for fasters in our setting may be that not eating what is set before us could lead others to stumble. For example, if it is during Lent and a friend serves me a steak when I visit his home, I should eat it. To say, "I'm sorry, but I'm fasting and can't eat this expensive meal that you've prepared. Could I have something else?" would be terribly rude and inconsiderate. I would tempt my brother to sin by showing disregard for his time, effort, and thoughtfulness. Better to eat what is set before me with thanksgiving. Love for other people is more important than keeping the letter of the law. And if it is well into Lent, you will really give thanks when you have to eat filet mignon.

The Lord told us to fast in secret, which means that we should draw as little attention to our self-denial as possible. In many settings, it is possible to order a vegetarian or vegan meal—or at least to have fish—without inconveniencing anyone or causing a scene. And if someone asks casually why we are having the salad and not the pot roast, it is fine to say, "Oh, I'm just lightening up a bit." Obviously, no one except a hermit can fast in total secrecy, but we should do our best to keep it to ourselves.

Of course, some close friends and family members will know about our Orthodox fasting discipline. So if I am going out to eat on a fast day with my college professor colleagues, I will usually suggest a place where I can have a decent meal within the guidelines, often an Oriental restaurant or a place with a vegetable plate or a salad bar. But if that is not possible for some reason, I just do the best I can and do not make a fuss. A few years ago, a friend really wanted to take me to his favorite hamburger place a few days before Christmas. His nephew was briefly in town and wanted to get my advice about graduate school. So I went along, had a hamburger with them, and then went back to the Advent fast. Our friendship and the opportunity to help the aspiring graduate student were more important than keeping the letter of the law that day.

A situation like that is similar to skipping your morning workout because someone needs your help or a friend really wants to meet you for breakfast. Your physical health probably will not suffer greatly as a result and some things are more important than the usual routine. Even in monasteries, hospitality may override ascetical strictness. Weary travelers need sustenance, even if the monks are on bread and water. You have to show love and concern for your guests, and making other people fast is not a virtue. If friends who do not fast in the Orthodox way come to our house for dinner during Lent, we serve something they will enjoy. It might be salmon, even though the guidelines generally allow only for shellfish during that strict season. But if we had a houseguest who was allergic to seafood and thought that all meals should include meat, as many Texans do, our dinner menu would reflect his preferences. Fasting is just a tool, while people are living icons of Christ. We put aside the tool of fasting when the Lord is present to us in another person whom we have the opportunity to serve.

It is beneficial to fast from anything with which we have an unhealthy relationship. A helpful test is to ask ourselves what our addictions are. Do we get upset whenever we do not get something in particular? Maybe it is grapefruit, chocolate cake, playing golf, checking Facebook obsessively, or following a set routine each day. Regardless of whether we are able to fast from food, it should be helpful to put some distance between ourselves and that activity or habit. Self-centered desires for pleasure take many forms and abstaining periodically from something that threatens to become a false god in our lives is always a good idea.

We do not fast from anything because it is evil, of course. Food, sex, and all the other blessings of creation are God's good work. The problem is not with them—it is with us. If we want to heal our broken relationship with them, we need to put our unhealthy longings in the back seat and our love for God in the front seat. In other words, it is time to direct our souls toward the Lord by taking a break from satisfying our addiction to getting what we want. Fasting creates space for God. Our ultimate satisfaction is in him. We turn from satisfying ourselves with false gods in order to turn to the one true God. That is the very heart of fasting.

One form of fasting in the Eastern Church is marital abstinence, when a married couple forgoes intercourse for a period of time as a way to fight their passions and devote more time and energy to prayer. St. Paul discusses this possibility in 1 Corinthians 7:5, noting that it should be done only for a brief period and by mutual consent. He states, "Do not deprive one another except with consent for a time, that you may give yourselves to fasting and prayer; and come together again so that Satan does not tempt you because of your lack of self-control." Well, it is not hard to imagine the evils that could come from one spouse denying sex to the other unilaterally or for a long period. Anger, resentment, adultery, divorce, etc., could easily be the result. Though the historic canons of the Orthodox Church call for marital fasting during Lent and other fasting periods, this discipline is applied pastorally for the salvation of particular couples. In other words, it is for those who are ready to embrace it in a healthy way; it is not imposed on anyone. The Orthodox Church does not attempt to regulate legalistically the intimate union of husband and wife. In normal pastoral practice, priests do not inquire about such details, unless there is a compelling reason to do so. If a couple would like guidance on some matter related to sex, they ask their priest in confidence.[5]

The marital fast is a reminder, however, that even the joyous union of husband and wife can become a false god and get in the way of our relationship with the Lord. Spouses can become mere sexual objects to one another. Marriage is to be an icon of the Kingdom, and it is good for man and woman to put aside even the joy of sex periodically to focus on the bliss of heaven. No, married sex is not evil in any way. Fasting is not about giving up bad things, but about distancing ourselves just a bit from good things that can get in the way because we have an unhealthy relationship with them.

That being said, some couples would do well to have intimate relations more often rather than less frequently. Instead of ignoring or depriving one another for petty or self-centered reasons, husbands and wives should joyfully embrace one another and the blessings of marriage. By its very nature, intercourse unites two people body and soul. The line of distinction between a husband and a wife is overcome in sexual intimacy; the two really do become one flesh. Here is an image of humanity as male and female in the image of God, united in love and potentially bringing forth new life. Christianity is not ashamed of the fact that we have bodies, that sex is pleasurable, or that God intended all this for our salvation. The vulnerability, intimacy, and joy of intercourse surely strengthen the bonds of love between spouses and help them to love Christ in one another.

Yes, marriage is a school in Christ-like love. We do not have to be married long at all before encountering opportunities to fight our passions. Forgiveness, patience, humility, generosity, selflessness, self-control, and fidelity are just a few of the virtues required for spouses in a healthy marriage. Not only do we accommodate our spouse, but also in-laws and

---

5. LeMasters, *The Goodness of God's Creation*, ch. 2.

usually kids. From changing diapers to arranging carpools and scrimping to pay for college, parenting helps us see that we are not isolated individuals but persons in relationship with others who are made for a common life of love. The sooner we get over the idea that we can think of ourselves apart from relationships with others, the better. God is a communion of persons: Father, Son, and Holy Spirit. We are created in that image. As strange as it may sound, a Christian sex life helps us grow into our salvation.

Another way that fasting from food, sex, or anything else helps us grow as Christians is in what it frees up for other uses. For example, if we are eating simply and less, we will probably have more money to give to needy people or the ministries of the Church. Jesus Christ said that if we do it to the least of these, we do it to him (Matt 25). People who do not worship their bellies will have more resources to offer the Lord in the poor and in the work of the Body of Christ. Our fast should become the poor person's feast. A toned down menu will often take less time to prepare than a big spread. When fasting from sex or other activities that require time and focus, we will have more energy to devote to prayer, Bible reading, helping others, and building healthy relationships.[6]

Some kids would gladly endure vegetable soup or peanut butter sandwiches for supper if that meant that mom and dad actually had time to play a game or simply talk with them before going to bed. Time normally spent watching a movie could be used to visit a lonely neighbor or someone in a nursing home. A married couple might actually discuss what's going on in their lives and how they can become better Christians together. Since prayer is our most fundamental way of developing a relationship with the Lord, we would all do well to cut out some distractions in our lives in order to have time to "be still and know that I am God"(Ps 46:10).

For those who are unable or unwilling to fast from food, turning aside from an unnecessary activity may serve the same end as disciplining the belly. Any time that we learn to redirect a focus on ourselves to a focus on God and our neighbors, we are the better for it. It is too bad that Adam and Eve learned that lesson the hard way. It is very good, however, that Jesus Christ has set right all that went wrong with our first parents. The fruit of the vine was our downfall, but he uses bread and wine to make us participants in his Body and Blood. The male-female relationship has been corrupted ever since Eden, but the Lord has made the wedding feast a sign of the Kingdom of God. Eating, drinking, making love, having babies, and

6. LeMasters, *The Goodness of God's Creation*, ch. 5.

joyfully learning to share the struggles of a common life together: these are among the paths to life eternal that the Savior has blessed. We learn to love God by offering these dimensions of our existence to him for fulfillment and transformation.

Some form of fasting is necessary to teach us that we really must offer ourselves to God if we want to enter into his joy. In order to avoid our inclination to gobble up all the goodies of creation for our own immediate enjoyment, we need some practice in saying "No!" to our self-centered desires for pleasure so that we can say "Yes!" to Jesus Christ. Fasting is a valuable Christian practice because it teaches us to do just that. But in order for it to be spiritually beneficial, we must fast in the proper context of prayer, humility, and secrecy. If we try to fast without prayer, we will run the risk of approaching this practice simply as something we accomplish by our own willpower, a work done to impress God and ourselves. If we fast without humility, we will judge others and congratulate ourselves on our superior spirituality. Pride will then steal whatever benefit we would have had from our self-control. Likewise, if we draw attention to our fasting, we will have our reward: the praise of other people. Read the section of the Sermon on the Mount on fasting before trying this at home (Matt 6:16–18). You will be glad you did.

As we grow in holiness and in union with God, we receive the strength to direct our desires to ever greater participation in the life and love of the Lord. Our longing for intimacy with a spouse becomes a sign of our deepening relationship with Christ. Our desire for food is a foreshadowing of our hunger for the blessings of the Heavenly Banquet. Fasting is a tool for purifying these desires, for setting right the distortions of appetite with which we are all too familiar in our corrupt world. If we want to get ready for the great feast of the Kingdom, some form of fasting is the way to go.

3

MARY: DON'T BE AFRAID!

IF IT IS CONTROVERSIAL in some quarters to refer to God as Father, it is equally—if not more—disturbing to many Christians to stress that Jesus Christ has a mother. In a knee-jerk reaction to the perception of an overemphasis on Mary in the Roman Catholic Church, many Protestants do their best to pay as little attention as possible to the first person to accept, love, and risk her life for the Son of God. Eastern Christianity finds that pretty strange. Our mothers play a crucial role in our life stories; no less is that the case for Jesus Christ. Only once does a member of the Holy Trinity become a human being, born of a woman (Gal 4:4). God surely does not play dice with the universe; who that woman was is very important.

Mary was a Jewish teenage girl, betrothed but not fully married, in a time and place where pregnancy out of wedlock was punishable by death. St. Luke's Gospel tell us that she responded with remarkable faith and obedience to the shocking message of the Archangel Gabriel that she was to be the virgin mother of the Messiah, even though—like everyone else—she could not rationally understand how that could happen. "Behold the handmaid of the Lord; let it be to me according to thy word" (Luke 1:38). In one of the most feminine and maternal scenes of the entire Bible, St. John the Baptist leaps in St. Elizabeth's womb at the presence of Jesus Christ, then in the womb of Mary (Luke 1:39–45). These two pregnant ladies are blessed to carry the Savior and his forerunner. Mary sings a song of praise to God for this good news, speaking boldly as a prophetess of how the Lord will put down the powerful and exalt the lowly. She predicts that "all generations will call me blessed" (Luke 1:48).

In the Eastern Church, Mary has the title *Theotokos*, which is Greek for "bearer of God" or "mother of God." No, she is not divine or the mother of the Holy Trinity, but Mary is truly the mother of Jesus Christ, one person who is both fully divine and fully human. Joseph, whom the Eastern Church remembers as an old man chosen against his will to be Mary's guardian, was understandably horrified at the news of the pregnancy, but he was reassured in a dream that the child was of the Holy Spirit. According to St. Matthew's Gospel, Joseph took Mary and Jesus to Egypt in order to escape a murder plot by King Herod, who did not want any rivals. Poor old Joseph did not spend his last years in peace, but at the center of the risk and danger that the Savior's unconventional conception and birth brought to the world (Matt 1:18–25).

Orthodox Christianity has honored Mary as Theotokos for as far back as anyone can tell. The title grew naturally from the worship of her son as also the Son of God. In the fourth century, a man named Nestorius refused to give Mary this title because he did not believe that the baby born to her was divine. He had no problem with honoring Mary as the mother of Jesus Christ, but he did not believe that the man Jesus was also the Son of God. In other words, he denied a true Incarnation. The Council of Ephesus in AD 431 denounced Nestorius's teachings, for only a Savior who is both fully God and fully divine can bring us humans into the eternal life of God. The Council also formally endorsed honoring Mary as the Theotokos, which Orthodox do in virtually every service of the Church.[1]

This story about Nestorius brings to light an important first lesson in understanding the Marian teaching of ancient Christianity. Namely, statements about Mary are in some ways teachings about Jesus Christ one step removed. In other words, our faith is obviously about Jesus Christ, the Son of God and our Savior. Mary receives special honor in the Church because of her unique role in the Incarnation, in how her Son came to be both God and man for our salvation. Those in ancient Christianity who balked at calling Mary the Theotokos or Mother of God did so, not because of reservations about Mary, but because of the refusal to confess that the human being Jesus Christ is also divine. By honoring Mary as the one who gave birth to the Son of God, the Eastern Church proclaims the mystery of our salvation in the God-Man. Yes, even he had a mother. God really did become a human being, born of a woman, in order to bring us into his life (Gal 4:4).

---

1. Alfeyev, *The Mystery of Faith*, 84–85, provides a discussion of Nestorius and the Council of Ephesus.

And she was not just any woman capable of carrying a pregnancy to term. The Fathers of the Eastern Church remember Mary as the New Eve, parallel to her Son, the New Adam. In order to understand this symbolism, recall that man and woman were created in God's image with the calling to grow ever more fully into the divine likeness. Unfortunately, our first parents chose to obey their own prideful will instead of the calling to grow in relationship with the Lord. The consequences of their taking a trajectory away from God are clear in the curses of Genesis: pain in childbirth and rule by her husband for the woman, with a life of sweat, toil, and ultimately death for the man (Gen 3:14–24). It is not a pretty picture, but more like one of those whiny George Jones songs. God does not abandon humanity, however; the drama of the Old Testament unfolds through generations of men and women who play their roles in preparing for the coming of a Messiah.

Mary is the high point, the fulfillment, of that preparation. As written in the *Protoevangelium of James* by the mid-second century, the Church remembers her parents as Joachim and Anna, an elderly, righteous, and barren couple who remind us of Abraham and Sarah.[2] God hears their prayer for a child like Samuel whom they will dedicate to God and who will live in the Temple in Jerusalem. That is where they take Mary as a young girl. The one who will become a living temple of God in her pregnancy grew up in the Temple, devoting herself to prayer and being fed by angels. Though she wanted to remain in the Temple all her days, that was impossible due to concerns about ritual purity and menstruation. When she had to leave the temple and to have a guardian, old Joseph came into the picture. I am always tempted to feel sorry for him at this point in the story. What old man—a widower who has already raised his children—would want to be bothered by the care of a teenage girl and then have to deal with the unbelievable news of a virgin birth? That is not much of a retirement, or even of just being left alone to putter around like old guys typically want to do.

Of course, this was not just any teenager. From as early as anyone can tell, ancient Christianity believed that Mary always said yes to God. She was a temple, righteous and pure, prepared as best as a human could be for union with the Lord. As a man, I cannot understand experientially the close bond between mother and child that pregnancy and nursing must bring. But I am sure that Mary was—and is—uniquely bonded to her Son.

---

2. Mathewes-Green, *The Lost Gospel of Mary*, has provided a translation of *The Protoevangelium of James* and other ancient Marian texts.

Unlike Roman Catholicism, the Eastern Church believes that Mary had to struggle with original sin.[3] In other words, she was born mortal into a world of spiritual and moral corruption where our self-centered desires run wild. Like everyone else, she had to resist temptation and surely would have found it easier to serve herself rather than God or neighbor. The amazing thing about Mary is that she never gave in to those temptations. She always obeyed the Lord and did not commit any actual sin. I do not understand rationally how she did that, but it is certainly understandable that God would choose the most righteous woman possible to become his living temple. Likewise, who else would have been able to say yes to the incredible assignment to become the Theotokos? As in so many areas of the faith, Orthodox believers are content to bow before the mystery affirmed by the Body of Christ.

Some of my evangelical friends will object at this point that someone who does not sin is not in need of a Savior. Fair enough, especially if salvation is simply a remedy for our sins. But what if salvation is about fulfilling our original calling to be like God, to become participants in the divine nature, and to be perfect as our Father in heaven is perfect? *Theosis* is not simply a matter of not breaking any laws; it concerns being so intimately united with the Lord that God's holiness becomes characteristic of who we are; it is sharing in the eternal life of the Holy Trinity by grace.

Even the most righteous Jew of the Old Testament could not conquer death or share in the fulfillment of God's promise in Jesus Christ. As righteous as she was, Mary certainly did not claim that she had somehow earned the unique glory of containing God in her womb, of becoming the living temple of the Most High. The Incarnation was not her idea. In humility, she gave thanks for his regard of her low estate, but was shocked and overwhelmed by the amazing message of the Archangel Gabriel. In obedience and purity, she found favor with God and was chosen from all women to play a distinctive, crucial role in the salvation of the world. But like everyone else, she needed a Savior; that is why she gave birth to him. The great thing about Mary is that she was able to say yes, to risk her life in order to play her role in the unfolding story of our salvation. She was not forced to become the mother of the Messiah. But in free obedience, she responded with purity of heart.

---

3. Gabriel, *Mary*, provides an excellent account of Orthodox teaching on the Theotokos, especially in contrast to Roman Catholic stances.

But why honor her with titles, hymns, icons, and feast days, as does the Orthodox Church? The book of Hebrews refers to a great cloud of witnesses that surrounds us as we pursue the Christian life (Heb 12:1). The Book of Revelation describes saints and martyrs who have gone before us to the heavenly throne (Rev 7: 9ff.). God sent the Archangel Gabriel to honor Mary: "Rejoice, highly favored one, the Lord is with you; blessed are you among women!" (Luke 1: 28) St. Elizabeth, pregnant with St. John the Baptist and filled with the Holy Spirit, also exclaims, "Blessed are you among women and blessed is the fruit of your womb" (Luke 1:42). Mary says of herself that "all generations will call me blessed" (Luke 1:48). When Orthodox Christians honor Mary, we are simply fulfilling her own prophecy and following the example of the Archangel Gabriel and of St. Elizabeth. The Theotokos stands at the head of the saints, of those who have shined brightly with God's holiness and gone on to be with him in the heavenly kingdom. Who could be closer to him than his own mother? How could we not honor the Theotokos for her unique role in our salvation, as well as all the saints for their powerful examples of keeping the faith alive across the generations?

The saints are like the members of the hall of fame. They are such good examples of the Christian life that we keep their memory alive, wanting to follow their examples of how to follow Jesus Christ. St. Paul wrote boldly to the Corinthians that they were to imitate him. He sent St. Timothy to them, "my beloved and faithful son in the Lord, who will remind you of my ways in Christ, as I teach everywhere in every church" (1 Cor 4:16–17). God's salvation is not an abstract concept, but the healing of a person in relationship with the communion of persons known as the Holy Trinity. So it makes perfect sense to look to the saints as exemplars of what it means for human beings to participate in the glory of God. They are witnesses that the salvation Christ brings to us is real and really does transform the lives of particular people.

There is no competition, of course, between honoring the saints and worshiping only the Lord. The famous teaching of Hebrews 12:1 about being "surrounded by so great a cloud of witnesses" is part of an exhortation to stay focused on Jesus Christ, "the author and finisher of our faith." The saints surround us like a crowd in a stadium cheering on their team or the spectators lining the streets during a long-distance race. They are not a distraction, but a source of encouragement to keep the faith and move forward toward the goal. They are living evidence that the Savior blesses, transforms, and heals human beings such that they shine with holiness. When we remember them, we are inspired to press forward with confident hope that God will glorify us also.

In addition, the Orthodox Church makes a formal distinction between veneration and worship. Veneration means honor, and we honor the saints with feast days, icons, hymns, readings, etc. However, we worship only God.[4] If that distinction does not make sense, consider what you would do if you heard your favorite public figure or sports hero give a rousing speech. More likely than not, you would stand up, applaud, and maybe even shout your approval. You might wait in line to get the person's autograph, buy a souvenir, and talk about the experience to everyone you met for a few days. If someone told you that you were an idolater because of your excitement over this celebrity, you would probably not agree. The same is true with how we stand up and salute the flag. Most people intuitively know that there is a difference between honoring those we admire and worshiping them as gods.

How Eastern Christianity honors Mary and the other saints may make the similarity harder to see, however. For example, Orthodox believers light candles before icons of holy people and kiss the icons, which may look like idolatry.[5] That is an understandable objection until we think about what we do with pictures of loved ones, such as departed family members. We are likely to put them in a prominent place, perhaps even one that is well lit or on the mantle above a fireplace, which creates much more light than a simple candle. We honor them by displaying their pictures prominently. A friend reports that deployed military members routinely kiss pictures of their spouses and loved ones. Of course, the pictures are not actually the people, but they are reminders of them. We direct our love their way by honoring visual images of them. And if anyone disrespected the pictures of our loved ones, we would take offense. It just seems to be human nature to ascribe a deep symbolic significance to people's images.

Another red flag for many people is praying to the saints. Since Christians are confident that God hears our prayers, why involve other people at all? Well, the first response is that it is perfectly uncontroversial to ask other people to pray for us. St. James writes that "The effective, fervent prayer

---

4. Webber, *Bread and Water, Wine and Oil*, comments, 107, that "The devotion belongs beyond the icon, and the veneration of the icon is always the veneration of the person or event depicted on it." See also Alfeyev, *The Mystery of Faith*, 112–15.

5. Classic writings in defense of Orthodoxy iconography include St. John of Damascus, *Three Treatises on the Divine Images*, and St. Theodore the Studite, *On the Holy Icons*.

of a righteous man avails much" (Jas 5:16). Those who have a particularly important prayer request, in any form of Christianity, will ask others to pray for them. They will probably especially ask those who seem righteous to appeal to the Lord on their behalf. Who better to serve as prayer warriors than the saints? They have completed the course and reached the goal of the heavenly Kingdom. The Book of Revelation describes heavenly worship, including at least a couple of references to the prayers of the saints as symbolized by incense (Rev 5:8, 8:4). The martyrs cry out, "'How long, O Lord, holy and true, until You judge and avenge your blood on those who dwell on the earth?'" (Rev 6:10). Even the rich man in Hades, who had neglected poor Lazarus, was concerned about the plight of his brothers on the earth (Luke 16:27–28).

The saints pray and are concerned with the fulfillment of God's purposes for humanity. There is one Church on earth and in heaven, one Body of Christ of which we are members. The saints cheer us on in the race for the Kingdom not only by their examples, but also by their active intercession on our behalf. That is why Orthodox Christians ask saints to pray for them. These requests for intercessory prayer never replace one's own prayers to the Lord, but are as much a part of the Christian life as asking a neighbor, friend, or pastor to put us on their prayer list.

Of course, some will object that the saints are dead and consequently not good prayer partners. The problem with that line of reasoning is that Christians believe that those who have died are with the Lord. When last I checked, all Christians worthy of the name believed in the resurrection. Christ's own promise to the thief on the cross, "Today you will be with me in Paradise" (Luke 23:43) as well as the portrait of Revelation, should ease those concerns. After all, what would we imagine that faithful Christians who have departed this life are doing? It makes sense to believe that they are worshiping and praying. I was surprised a few years ago when an acquaintance bemoaned the passing of a righteous friend with the comment that she could no longer pass along prayer requests to her. She was even more surprised when I suggested that her friend is surely now in an even better position to intercede for her with the Father.

Of all the saints, the Theotokos is the most powerful intercessor, the greatest prayer warrior of them all.[6] If that seems like an odd thing to say, remember how the Lord came to perform his first miraculous sign in St. John's Gospel, of turning water into wine. He did so because his mother

---

6. See Mathewes-Green, *The Lost Gospel of Mary*, ch. 2.

asked him to (John 2:1ff.). Jesus Christ is fully divine and fully human, and all healthy human beings have a special affection for their mothers. The same is apparently true of him. So we should not be surprised that the experience of the Orthodox Church is that the Son still listens with particular attention to his mother's requests. If that makes the Lord sound too human, all the better. He remains fully divine and fully human, even in heaven where he is seated at the right hand of the Father.

The ongoing experience of Orthodox Christians is also important for understanding the veneration of the Theotokos and the other saints. Throughout the history of the Church, there are numerous accounts of people asking her to pray for them and then receiving what they requested. No, this is not a simplistic "name it" and claim it theology, but it is an ongoing experience of Eastern Christians that her prayers are especially effective. Otherwise, the practice of asking for her intercessions, and those of other saints, would surely have died out long ago.[7]

Everyone in the Orthodox Church venerates the Theotokos, but women often have a special attachment to her. That is not surprising because it is precisely in her femininity that she played a crucial role in our salvation which no male could ever play. The most honored saint is a woman and a mother, which stands as a powerful reminder that God's holiness is not the exclusive possession of biological males. I ask for Mary's intercessions as part of my daily rule of prayer, but especially request her prayers for my wife Paige and daughters Kate and Annie. Who better to help them through the trials and tribulations of life than this uniquely glorified woman? She understands the challenges they face far better than I do.

My impression is that virtually every culture has failed in at least some ways to value women's gifts, interests, and experiences. Pregnancy, childbirth, childrearing, and domestic work are often kept out of sight and out of mind by the powerful of any society. When we remember that Jesus Christ really did have a mother and that she was the first to love, accept, and serve him, those culturally biased assumptions are challenged. Our best example of a human being in communion with God is Mary, an unmarried teenage virgin when chosen by him for a mission beyond anyone's understanding. The old priest Zachariah balked at the less astounding news that he and Elizabeth would conceive in old age. (Hadn't he heard of Abraham and Sarah?) But with amazing purity and obedience, Mary said yes and

---

7. See Sakharov, *Saint Silouan the Athonite*, 390–98, for Saint Silouan's account of the ongoing role of the Theotokos and the Saints in the lives of Christians.

became the living temple of God. She is the most blessed among women and a model for all humanity in how to accept Christ into our lives. If anyone doubts that women may exceed men in holiness, let them ponder the spiritual glory of Mary the Theotokos.

It may be puzzling, then, that the Orthodox Church does not ordain women to the priesthood, not even Mary. Christ's apostles were males, and they became the first bishops of the early Church who passed on their ministry by the laying on of hands to the next generation of male leaders. Eastern Christianity did have the office of deaconess in the early centuries, however. These were ministers whose work seems to have been focused largely on women when there were cultural barriers to male ministers visiting women's homes or baptizing undressed females. That office fell out of use, though there are efforts to restore it today. As best I can tell, the debate about bringing back female deacons is now not so much theological as practical.[8]

The issue of women priests is a bit different. Some Orthodox argue that an exclusively male priesthood reflects the particularity of the Incarnation, as Jesus Christ was male and the priest represents him in the liturgy and sacraments of the Church. For example, a female would normally have the role of Mary in a Christmas pageant; likewise, a male has the role of Christ in priestly ministry. An icon of the Theotokos portrays her as a female, while the icon of the Lord presents a male human being. Others will point out that the experience of the Church has always been of a male priesthood, which is compatible with the masculine imagery of the Father and the Son. The Church is the bride of Christ and he is the groom. Gender is part of the mystery of personhood; though many find it naïve today, Eastern Christianity does not think that fathers and mothers are either identical or interchangeable. The same is true of husbands, wives, sons, and daughters. The Church has always known its priests as spiritual fathers. They are addressed as "Father" and typically wear beards. Christ's priesthood has been exercised from the origins of the Orthodox Church by males.[9]

Though there are a small number of advocates for the ordination of women to the priesthood in Orthodoxy, the role of women in the Church is not nearly as controversial in the East as it is in Protestant and Roman

---

8. Farley, *Feminism and Tradition*, ch. 5, cautions against the restoration of the female diaconate.

9. See Mathewes-Green, "Women's Ordination, " para. 12.

Catholic circles.[10] Perhaps part of the reason for that is the robust ministry of women throughout the history of the Church.[11] For example, St. Mary Magdalene and several other women have the title of "Equal to the Apostles" because they were such powerful evangelists. Virtually every Sunday, the Church sings about the myrrh-bearing women who bravely went to the tomb to anoint the dead Jesus, while the male disciples apparently cowered in fear. A Sunday in Lent is devoted to the example of St. Mary of Egypt, a former prostitute who became an example of repentance, asceticism, and holiness.[12] The twentieth-century Saint Maria Skoptsova led efforts to hide Jews from the Nazis in Paris and died as a result in a concentration camp, by some reports taking the place of another prisoner in the gas chamber.[13] One of the most popular Orthodox authors and speakers in America today is a woman named Frederica Mathewes-Green. The wife of a priest, she's an evangelist and cultural critic whose books, podcasts, and lectures have brought many men and women into Eastern Christianity.

Several times throughout the year, the Church celebrates feast days of the Theotokos. Even in a church led by bearded bishops and priests, women are quite prominent. It is impossible to avoid the central role of the Theotokos in Orthodoxy, as her icon is prominently displayed in every parish. Usually, a church's iconography includes several of her and of other women saints. The Church highlights the holiness, leadership, and ministry of women in many ways. Women teach in Orthodox seminaries and serve as chairpersons of boards of Orthodox organizations, schools, and ecclesiastical departments. In women's monasteries, the abbess (the head nun) is clearly in charge, even overseeing the priests who visit to conduct services. Currently in my congregation, our parish council chairperson, treasurer, iconographer, and head chanter are all women. As is the case in all Christian churches, most ministries would shut down without the dedicated efforts of the women who do lots, if not most, of the work.

No, Mary was not a priest, but she is the Theotokos, the living temple of God, whom Orthodoxy believes to have followed her Son body and soul

---

10. For a variety of perspectives, see: Farley, *Feminism and Tradition*; Limouris, *The Place of the Woman in the Orthodox Church and the Question of the Ordination of Women*; Hopko, *Women and the Priesthood*; and Behr-Sigel, *The Ministry of Women in the Church*.

11. See FitzGerald, *Encountering Women of Faith*, and Tkacz, "Women and the Church in the New Millennium," 243–74.

12. "Medieval Sourcebook: The Life of our Holy Mother Mary of Egypt."

13. Hackel, *Pearl of Great Price*, provides an account of the life of this remarkable saint.

into the Kingdom after her death. Three days after her death, what we call the Dormition (or falling asleep) of the Theotokos, her tomb was found to be empty. She did not return to life in this world, but was the first to share in her Son's victory over death. Mary was also the first to accept Christ into her life and the only one joined intimately to him as flesh and blood. The Eastern Church sings Mary's praises in beautiful, poetic terms, using the language of love for our "undisputed intercessor," whose womb became "more spacious than the heavens" when she carried within her the eternal Son of God. In Mary the uniquely feminine experiences of pregnancy and motherhood are taken up into the good news of our salvation, which could not have occurred without the consent of a young woman so righteous that she was able to say "yes."

A church that was ashamed of women or wanted to oppress them would not remember Mary in this way as the ideal Christian who played a crucial role in the Incarnation. Neither would it highlight St. Mary Magdalene as the one who first preached the good news of the resurrection to the doubting male disciples. The title "Equal to the Apostles" would apply only to males in a church that thought women had no role in ministry. The veneration of the Theotokos exalts the role of women, even as it recognizes that the biological differences between the sexes are theologically relevant. There is no Gnostic escape from the body here, for no male could have played Mary's role. Precisely as a woman, a mother, and a virgin, she is a living embodiment of what God can do through the life of a human being. In this sense, she is a model for us all. Mary is a living icon of our salvation, truly the living temple of the Lord.

Orthodox Christians call the Theotokos "the Virgin Mary" because we believe that she was a virgin when she conceived Christ by the Holy Spirit and that she remains eternally a virgin. In the memory of the Church, Joseph was an older relative chosen against his will be Mary's guardian. This teaching does not imply that married sex is evil, but instead that Mary had a special role as the living temple of God. The references to Christ's brothers and sisters have always been taken in Eastern Christianity to refer to the widowed Joseph's children from a previous marriage. Likewise, the reference in St. Matthew's Gospel to Joseph not knowing his wife until Jesus's birth is a way of stressing that Joseph was not the biological father of the Lord (Matt 1:24–25). The Greek word for "until" is the same as that used for "I will be with you always until the end of the word" (Matt 28:20). The point is not that Christ will abandon his people at the end of the world, but instead to stress that he will be with them throughout their time in the world as we know it. Likewise, the Lord's words from the cross to St. John, "Son, behold your mother," and to Mary, "Woman, behold your son," would have made no sense had Mary had other biological children (John 19:26–27). They would have cared for her in her old age and widowhood. But since Christ was her only child, he had to entrust her to St. John's care.[14]

A friend tells me that she has trouble accepting the perpetual virginity of Mary because the teaching implies to her a low view of marriage. In other words, the sexual union of husband and wife must be somehow evil if Mary and Joseph did not participate in it. The concern is understandable, but the issue at stake is not the general status of intercourse between husband and wife. It is, instead, the uniqueness of the Incarnation of the Son of God. The Church's memory of Mary is that she became the Theotokos, the living temple of the Lord. She gave birth miraculously to one child who was also God. This was not her plan or Joseph's, but they faithfully fulfilled the callings that they received. She was and remains eternally a virgin as the New Eve through whom salvation came to the world.

The Lord's birth is not part of the usual ongoing story of human corruption and death, neither is it connected to our inevitably disordered sexual desires. Instead, it is entirely miraculous and without precedent or sequel in the history of the universe. Mary was the chosen vessel for the miracle and lived out her life in virginal purity because that is who she was: a human being totally open to, dependent upon, and dedicated to the Lord. It is not as though a bunch of theologians got together and introduced belief in her perpetual virginity because they did not like sex. As far back as anyone can tell, this was the faith of the early Christians. It is how the Church has always remembered the Virgin Mary.

My Protestant friends are sometimes surprised to learn that Martin Luther, John Calvin, Ulrich Zwingli, and John Wesley all believed in the perpetual virginity of Mary.[15] Before the Protestant Reformation, hardly anyone questioned this teaching. In talking with skeptical friends over the years, I have become comfortable with the conclusion that the Church teaches this point about Mary simply because we believe that it is true. Had it somehow been otherwise, Christ would still be our Savior. The point here is not abstract theological necessity, but faithfulness to what the Holy Spirit has revealed.

---

14. Mathewes-Green, *The Lost Gospel of Mary*, 19–20; and Gabriel, *Mary*, 41ff.
15. Herfurth, "The *Theotokos*," 23ff.; Wesley, "A Letter to a Roman Catholic."

"Revealed where?" some readers may ask. It is sometimes objected that the scriptures do not explicitly instruct us to venerate Mary or the other saints, neither do they define her sinlessness or perpetual virginity in black and white. From the perspective of Eastern Christianity, that is not a problem because the Bible is not the only witness to God's truth. Something does not have to be taught clearly in the scriptures in order to be true. Orthodoxy seeks to be faithful to the fullness of the tradition, to what has been handed down from the time of the apostles through the life of the people of God. The saints, creeds, decrees of councils, icons, hymns, prayers, liturgical services, etc., are all part of how the Holy Spirit has led the Church. These different manifestations of tradition do not contradict one another, but together enrich our understanding. The Orthodox perspective is that no equivalent of the Protestant Reformation has ever been necessary in Eastern Christianity because the Church has not developed traditions contrary to the genuine faith.

For most people who become Orthodox from a Protestant background, giving so much attention to Mary and to the other saints is often a bit of a struggle at first. It is so different from what we experienced in other churches and may seem totally misguided at first glance. I have to admit that I did not understand, and had not even seriously studied, the rationale for Catholic or Orthodox veneration of Mary until I was on my way to becoming Orthodox several years after finishing a PhD in theology.

Like many endeavors in life, this is an observance with which people become more comfortable over time as they grow into it. By making sign of the cross, lighting a candle, kissing her icon, and then asking for the Theotokos's intercessions, Orthodox believers become accustomed to honoring Mary and asking for her prayers, both for themselves and for others. Prayer is always a mystery; I have never met anyone with a formula to explain exactly how it works. Likewise, there is much about the intercessions of the saints that is well beyond our full comprehension. But just as we trust that God hears the prayers of our faithful friends in this life, Eastern Christians trust that God hears the prayers of holy people departed this life and that their prayers are quite powerful.

A former student and good friend who is a Protestant minister once told me that he simply could not begin to make sense of Marian devotion. I responded that he really had to get to know the Theotokos in order to begin to appreciate the practice. He laughed, but I was serious. So I gave him an Orthodox prayer book and suggested that he start to ask for Mary's intercessions to the extent that he felt comfortable doing so. A few weeks later, he closed the door to his office and said, "It worked!" It's good to know that at least one Methodist elder is getting to know the Mother of God.

Mary is also our mother, for we are members of Christ's Body, the Church. Her Son lives in the hearts of his followers; we are in Christ. So she is our mother also, eager to help us experience more fully the blessedness for which we were created. The more we get to know her, the better we will know Jesus Christ. Yes, there is a family resemblance. And the more we come to resemble Mary the Theotokos, the better. In virtually all Orthodox icons that portray her, Mary is with Christ. She presents her Son to us, pointing to him as the Savior. Her example reminds us that we are also called to become his living temples and to play our role in making his salvation present in the world. Who better to be our example than the very first human being who accepted Christ into her life? Who better to pray for us? There is no reason to be afraid of honoring his and our mother.

4

FOOTBALL, LITURGICAL WORSHIP, AND REAL LIFE

A STRANGE THING HAPPENS on Friday nights from August through December in Texas. Otherwise sane people drive for hours; sit or stand for even more hours in blazing heat, fierce winds, and bitter cold; cheer, jeer, and scream at teenagers and referees; and then drive back home, often arriving in the wee hours of the morning. It is the highlight of the week and an endeavor so important that school, work, family, and church often take a back seat to it. Yes, it is Texas high school football. *Friday Night Lights* is all too accurate. (Sometimes these rituals also occur on Thursday or Saturday nights.) As a native Texan who gave up football after junior varsity, I have at least some level of sympathy for these excesses. Paige and I have season tickets for Abilene High and I go to a few home games each year, but am not really a traveling fan.

At the risk of giving the impression that I played too much without a helmet, Friday night football is actually a good place to begin explaining Orthodox worship and its relationship to how we live the rest of the week. The main service of worship on Sundays and other feast days is the Divine Liturgy, the work of the people in worshiping God. Including the preparatory morning prayers, known as Matins, the Sunday morning services in a typical parish last at least two hours and often three of more. (Vespers, evening prayer, is usually conducted the night before for about an hour.) The length of Liturgy will depend upon how many people take Communion, what musical arrangements the choir and chanters are singing, and whether or not there are additional prayers or processions according to the calendar of the church year. Services in Lent are among the longest.

Eastern Christian worship takes a long time and a lot of effort. As the sister of one of our parishioners once said, "Just to make it through the service is an ascetic struggle." How true. People stand up for much of the time, like the ancient Christians who did not have pews and rose to honor God in their prayers. Many parishes in North America do have pews, but the people still stand much more than in a typical Protestant service. The choir, chanters, people, and priest sing the entire service. Football games are similar with devoted fans on their feet shouting much of the time. I knew I was back in Texas my first year at McMurry when I heard an innocent looking coed scream "kill him!" with all her might several times during a game. Though we do not yell such violent slogans during Liturgy, everyone vocalizes their reason for being there: the worship of God.

The church is filled with beautiful icons and the sweet smell of incense permeates the atmosphere. Parishioners make the sign of the cross many times. During Sunday Matins they normally come forward to kiss a bejeweled book containing the readings from the Gospels. After Liturgy, they kiss a cross that the priest holds in his hand. Orthodox liturgy is a multimedia endeavor that appeals to all five senses. I have noticed that even high school stadiums in my part of the world now fill the senses with video playing on the score board, fake smoke surrounding the team as they take the field, and an ongoing battle of the bands throughout the contest. Cheerleaders, drill teams, and band members—as well as the players, of course—wear glitzy uniforms. Some fans paint their faces, while many more don their school colors and sometimes wave homemade signs to inspire the players. Yes, it is a sight to behold.

Though some parishes do have organs, Orthodox music is typically sung a cappella. It is not that it is a sin to use a piano, but the Church's musical experience is an extension of the ancient chants of Judaism performed by the one instrument created directly by God, the human voice. Orthodox liturgical music is not so much performed as prayed. Ideally, the chanters, choir, and people all sing out the praise of God, using ancient lyrics and Byzantine or Russian-style arrangements that have been blessed by the voices of generations of believers. In small parishes like my own, we do not have a choir, so the chanters and the brave souls in the pews sing the services together.

Like fans driving across the vast open spaces of Texas, parishioners sometimes travel long distances to our church, including three families at St. Luke who come in from small towns out in the country. All that the members of our parish really have in common is their faith. Our small membership includes: Air Force personnel, a corrections officer, a deputy sheriff, a fireman, some retirees, a physician, a lawyer, a professor, school teachers, a customer service representative at a bank, a nurse's aide, the manager of a trucking firm, a couple of college students, and a few other assorted folks together with their kids. Our places of origin include: Romania, Greece, Africa, various Texas towns, and even that distant and strange land known as New York. We live in different neighborhoods and towns, have divergent levels of education and income, and widely different personalities and interests. Were it not for our common faith, most of us would never have met even in a place the size of Abilene.

Like the spectators at an athletic event, however, we take on a shared identity when we gather publicly to serve something (in this case, Someone) larger than ourselves. We are the Church, the Body of Christ, in communion with people around the world who believe, worship, and seek to live as Orthodox Christians. This communion extends even beyond this world to include that great cloud of witnesses that have finished the race together with all the heavenly host. We do not paint our faces or twirl terrible towels or yell "kill him!," but we do become a new community that together prays, proclaims a shared faith, and takes Communion. Instead of the tomahawk chop, we make the sign of the cross and bow down making prostrations before the Lord. In place of uniforms, the clergy and altar servers wear vestments that reflect the divine glory of heavenly worship. They do not stand at the altar in their workaday duds, even as players on the field do not. They have a special role to play that is not of this world.

In the Baptist congregation in which I was raised, the pastor wore a robe (white, if I remember) only when he conducted baptisms. He normally wore a suit to preach and I know that many Protestant clergy today dress casually to lead worship. In contrast, Orthodox priests wear at least some vestments over black robes in all services. For the Divine Liturgy, we don a full array of vestments colored to reflect the season of the church year. My experience is that the vestments take the attention off the personality of the priest and direct our focus to Jesus Christ, our Great High Priest. If congregants are curious to see where I buy my suits and how worn they are or if I have good taste, they are falling prey to distraction. And if a pastor wastes time with those concerns, he is doing the same thing. But if we wear the vestments we wear them because that is what Orthodox priests do, and if the vestments are so stylized that they do not fit conventional notions of fashion anyway, there likely will be much less self-consciousness and distraction. Just imagine how much less focus there would be on the football game if players wore whatever they liked on the field. In football and most other sports, that would create chaos. Once the attire is set, we can attend to more important matters in athletics or the church.

The priest presides in the Liturgy as a representative of Christ by virtue of ordination and the gifts of the Holy Spirit conveyed through the laying on of hands by the bishop, not his own personal charisma. When you see a clergyman wearing some version of the same vestments as all other clergymen, the impression is more: "It's time to worship God!" than "It's time for the Father Philip show!" As well, it is quite humbling to wear vestments. Each piece of clothing is put on with certain prayers, and it is basically dressing up like Christ in order to become a liturgical icon or symbol of him. The priest stands at Christ's altar, gives the people his peace and blessing, and even serves them his Body and Blood. No, it is not my show in any sense. More than anything else, the vestments remind me of my unworthiness to minister in his name.

Fans at a football game know that a certain schedule will be followed. They show up early to get a program and watch the pre-game warm-ups; then stand and cheer as the team takes the field; then stand and sing for the national anthem and school song, and bow their heads for the moment of silence. Then there are two quarters, the half time show, and the last two quarters. Trips to the concession stand and to the restroom usually fit in somewhere also. Fans of some teams have particular traditions about when to stand up, sit down, shake their keys for a "key play," what to yell at the referees when they flub a call, etc.

We become better fans by learning more about the sport, going to games, following the team, and putting our hearts into cheering them on. My Beaumont-Charlton-Pollard High School was the product a merger of a white and a black school for the sake of racial integration in the 1970s. BCP later morphed again into another institution with a different name. Consequently, we had few school traditions and alums have no team to support. In contrast, Paige's Midland High continues to play the same teams it played when she was a student. Her mother, sisters, and brother-in-law went there also. Midland is in the same athletic distract as Abilene, so she endures the same annoying "Mojo" chants from Odessa Permian fans and the playing of "Dixie" by the Midland Lee band. (No, that was not a popular song at my high school.) These are living traditions that shape how people think, feel, and act concerning sports, school, communities, and themselves. Fans become characters in a narrative that began before they were born and will continue beyond them. (I do not have a high school to cheer for, but as an undergraduate at Baylor became part of "that good old Baylor line." Sic'em Bears!)

We normally do not judge athletic contests by how they make us feel or whether we get something out of them that helps us through the week or to find peace for our personal problems. Instead, we enter into their excitement and struggle, leaving our normal identities and preoccupations behind in order to embrace a distinctive communal experience much larger than ourselves. The popularity of spectator sports indicates that doing so appeals to many people at a deep level. No one would suggest eliminating the third quarter or making a touchdown count for four points simply due to personal preference. And barring lightning strikes, the game will go on—no matter who gets hurt, how much it rains, how truly miserable we are sitting exposed to the elements, or how well the teams are doing. Above all, respect the game if you want to be a fan.

The similarities to liturgical worship are obvious. Eastern Christianity follows orders of worship that have their origins in the temple and synagogue services of the Jews. The early Christians adopted those Hebraic patterns and added the Eucharist at the end. St. Justin Martyr's description of worship in the second century follows the same general patterns that we see elaborated more fully in the Divine Liturgies of Sts. Basil the Great and John Chrysostom, the two versions of the Liturgy used to this day in the Eastern Orthodox Church on Sundays and for major feasts.[1] Though there continued to be development in the details for a few centuries, the services of the Orthodox Church are ancient and set.[2] While there will probably always be small differences in how various services are conducted in different parts of the world or different ecclesiastical jurisdictions, all Orthodox pray the same liturgies.[3] Whether in Greece, Russia, Lebanon, or Texas, Eastern

---

1. Justin Martyr, "The First Apology of Justin," LXV-LXVII, as cited in Roberts and Donaldson, *Ante-Nicene Fathers* 1, 185–86, and Ware, *The Orthodox Church*, 28off.

2. Williams and Anstall, *Orthodox Worship*, 56–57. and Wybrew, *The Orthodox Liturgy*, 13ff.

3. There are a small number of Orthodox parishes that worship according to the Western Rite, which refers to older Catholic and Anglican services that have been

Christians are playing the same game with just a bit of local variation, not unlike teams in different locations in the same league.

The focus of Orthodox worship is not on entertaining or even inspiring those in attendance, however. The focus is on God, specifically on worshiping him. It is about something larger than ourselves. He is the Alpha and the Omega of the universe, the great "I AM" of the burning bush who is even more important to believers than football is to Texans. The vast majority of the time during Liturgy and the other services, the priest stands facing the altar with his back to the people. The point is not to ignore them, but to lead the congregation in prayer and worship. He stands at the front of the pack. Of course, the priest faces the congregation to read the Gospel lesson, preach the sermon or homily, bless and give Christ's peace to the people, and serve Communion. But otherwise, he prays at the altar. Orthodox clergy are actually expected to worship during the services. The focus is not on the popularity or eloquence of their sermons or their ability to inspire action or emotions in the hearts of parishioners. Instead, it is on offering God the service and worship that are due him simply because he is God.

Mentioning the sermon reminds me that Eastern Christian worship does not revolve around it. Homilies are usually fairly short pastoral talks on the Gospel or epistle passage for the day, the saint being commemorated, or a theme related to where we are in the Church's calendar year. The Liturgy is a service of worship that we offer to the Lord, not primarily a time for the people to be instructed or inspired. In many Protestant services, the quality of the service boils down to the quality of the sermon, which can be quite long, even well beyond the attention span of the average adult. Though the Orthodox Church has had its share of great preachers such as St. John Chrysostom, not even the best speech can compare to the beauty and spiritual profundity of the Divine Liturgy. To stay with the sports analogy, a great discourse by a famous coach is of interest to fans, but that is not why they go to the stadium. Likewise, the Orthodox Church gathers to enter into the worship of heaven and participate in the Wedding Feast of the Lamb. A speech with a couple of preparatory songs simply will not cut it.

I have heard another Orthodox priest say that the point of Orthodox music and art is not that we will change them, but that they will change us. The same is true of worship. God prescribed in the Old Testament how the

---

changed slightly in order to conform to Orthodox theological norms. The overwhelming majority of Orthodox parishes follow the Byzantine Rite, however.

Jews were to worship him. The early Christians were Jews who followed that pattern and added Communion.[4] One of the meanings of the word "Orthodoxy" is right worship. There is an old saying in Latin that the rule of prayer is the rule of belief. In other words, how any group worships manifests what it believes. Eastern Christians accept these liturgical traditions as part of God's truth handed down in the Body of Christ by the power of the Holy Spirit. God is Holy Mystery and embracing his life is a participatory event, the growth and deepening of a relationship with him. The Lord has worked through these services for two thousand years to make saints and to preserve and manifest the fullness of the faith. We are to grow into them, to be shaped by their sounds, smells, sights, and practices. If sports fans have to work in order to advance in their love and knowledge of the game, the same is true for us.

It is even more true because the Church does not gather for the passing goals of entertainment, athleticism, or building community spirit, but truly to participate in the Wedding Feast of the Lamb, the Heavenly Banquet. Like the man in the parable, we need to put on our wedding garments and get with the program, otherwise we will not be prepared to take part in the celebration (Matt 22:1–14). To have the attitude that worship is valid only if it makes me feel a certain way or suits my ascetic sensibilities is terribly wrongheaded and even more spiritually dangerous. Worship is about entering into the holiness of God as member of Christ's Body. The Prophet Isaiah was overwhelmed by a sense of unworthiness in his vision of the heavenly temple (Isa 6:5). He did not suggest to the Almighty that the furniture be rearranged or that there be less smoke or more hymns that he really liked. The set liturgical worship of Eastern Christianity helps to take the focus off ourselves and our preferences. It fosters humility and repentance, for who are we to participate in such divine glory? The prayers, services, and hymns passed down by generations of holy men and women, including martyrs, are a cherished heritage. We have no right to change them to suit our tastes.

Athletes prepare in a disciplined way for a season and for each game. Likewise, Orthodox who intend to take Communion during a given Liturgy say prayers of preparation the night before. They also abstain from marital relations that evening and from food and drink after midnight. Let's be very clear: there is nothing sinful about intercourse between husband and wife or about eating and drinking. But as we prepare for the great Wedding

4. Williams and Anstall, *Orthodox Worship*, chs. 1–2.

Feast, we put aside all distractions so that we will be focused and ready. Married sex is not dirty or evil, but it may well turn our attention away from intense prayer.[5] If we really want to enjoy a big dinner, we should be good and hungry when we finally sit at the dining table. In the same way, we put off our usual food and drink in order to be focused on the miraculous joy of receiving the Body and Blood of Christ, the medicine of immortality. We fast so that we may feast. None of this preparation makes us worthy to receive the Eucharist. Indeed, the main theme of the preparatory prayers is precisely our need for Christ's mercy and forgiveness because we are so unworthy of him.

St. Paul emphasized our need to prepare for Communion quite strongly in 1 Corinthians 11:27–30:

> Therefore whoever eats this bread or drinks this cup of the Lord in an unworthy manner will be guilty of the body and blood of the Lord. But let a man examine himself, and so let him eat of the bread and drink of the cup. For he who eats and drinks in an unworthy manner eats and drinks judgment to himself, not discerning the Lord's body. For this reason many are weak and sick among you, and many sleep.

That is serious business, especially since "sleep" in that sense is literally death! Yes, St. Paul is saying that to receive the Eucharist unprepared is very serious business that we should avoid at all costs.

If Orthodox believers are aware of any serious sin in their lives or have a guilty conscience, they should take confession before receiving Communion. Most people do well to confess every couple of months. The point is not legalism, but healing. Confession is therapeutic for the soul sickened and weakened by sin. The Risen Jesus gave his disciples the authority to declare the forgiveness of sins in St. John's Gospel (John 20:21–23). That ministry continues in the Orthodox Church through the work of priests who assure penitents of God's forgiveness and give them advice for turning away from sin and to the Lord. Of course, the priest has no magical powers; the person taking confession who is not truthful or repentant reaps more spiritual disease than health.

All Orthodox, including bishops and priests, take confession, which the clergyman must keep absolutely confidential. I have learned from experience that there is a great freedom found in naming my sins aloud to God and being told by another human being that all is forgiven. And it is

---

5. LeMasters, *The Goodness of God's Creation*, 41ff.

not by any random human being, but a priest who is set apart and gifted for this ministry by the Holy Spirit. He is also committed to confidentiality and formed spiritually and intellectually to discern how to guide his spiritual children. There are disciplinary canons that describe the gravity of and appropriate remedy for various sins, especially grave matters like murder, adultery, and abandoning the Christian faith. While priests take them into account in advising penitents, they apply them pastorally toward the spiritual healing of the particular person in question. There is not so much a legal as a therapeutic approach to confession in Eastern Christianity.

Some of the words in the prayers said by the priest in Confession usually stop me in my tracks because they are so profound and powerful. They place our common situation as sinners squarely in the context of the Lord's mercy. If we are truly repentant, we put away obsessive guilt by trusting in his forgiveness. For example,

> I, humble and a sinner, have not power on earth to forgive sins, but God alone; yet through that divinely spoken word which came to the Apostles after the resurrection of our Lord Jesus Christ . . . Whatsoever thou hast said to my most humble self, and whatsoever thou hast not succeeded in saying, either through ignorance, or through forgetfulness, whatever it may be: God forgive then in this present world and in that which is to come.
>
> God . . . who forgave David through Nathan the Prophet, when he confessed his sins, and Peter weeping bitterly for his denial, and the sinful woman in tears at his feet, and the Publican, and the Prodigal Son: May that same God forgive thee all things, through me a sinner, both in this present world, and in that which is to come, and set thee uncondemned before his dread Judgment Seat. And now, having no further care for the sins which thou has declared, depart in peace.[6]

As in all the sacraments, the priest hearing confession is a living icon of Christ through whom the Lord makes present his mercy to sinners. Some people object to confession because they believe that the Christian life is an individualistic effort, a form of "Jesus and me" spirituality in which we are all self-sufficient before the Lord. That is more a Western cultural sentiment than a genuinely Christian one. I have reminded skeptical students that we do not evangelize or baptize ourselves, conduct our own weddings or Communion services, or provide our own pastoral counseling. God works through other members of the Church to minister to us in those ways.

---

6. *A Pocket Prayer Book for Orthodox Christians*, 44–45.

Likewise, St. James's instruction to "confess your trespasses to one another, and pray for one another that you may be healed" (Jas 5: 16) challenges severely the individualistic assumption that my sins concern only me and that I may find healing from them all by myself. We will look in vain for any passage in the Bible that presents confession of sin as a solitary matter between the individual and God.

It is true both physically and spiritually. "And if one member suffers, all the members suffer with it . . . " (Rom 12:26). If that is hard to believe, my chiropractor and massage therapist will give testimony. I need their help to stretch, straighten, and do other uncomfortable things to my muscles and joints. A herniated disk and a bit of arthritis here and there can ruin your whole day and impact the way the entire body functions and how we treat others. Just a little bit of discomfort unfortunately tends to make me rather unpleasant to be around. Since it is beyond my ability to address these problems without the help of trained professionals, I do several weird stretches the chiropractor gave me and submit myself to the sometimes painful kneading of the massage therapist. So far, so good.

When any member of the Church is weakened and sickened by sin, the whole Body struggles as a result. It is like St. Paul's image in 1 Corinthians 5:6–8 of Jews sweeping leaven out of their kitchens for Passover. Just a little yeast is disastrous for someone trying to make unleavened bread. A chain is only as strong as its weakest link, and the debilitating presence of spiritual or moral corruption in the life of a believer weakens the entire Church. Our sins are not only our business, but a legitimate concern of the Body of Christ. So with absolute confidentiality, we bare our souls to the Lord in the presence of a priest who guides us toward greater spiritual health, praying for us and assuring us of God's forgiveness. In his earthly ministry, Jesus Christ forgave everyone who came to him in humble repentance. In Confession, we are assured that he still does.

The highpoint of the Divine Liturgy is the miraculous transformation of bread and wine into the Body and Blood of Christ. Orthodox who have prepared themselves by prayer, fasting, and confession come forward near the end of the service to receive "the precious and all-holy Body and Blood of our Lord, God, and Savior Jesus Christ, unto the forgiveness of sins and life everlasting." The priest administers the sacrament personally to each communicant, saying the person's name as he puts a small portion of the Eucharist into his or her open mouth with a special spoon. We serve communion even to little babies, for they too have put on Christ in baptism and been filled with the Holy Spirit in chrismation. (Chrismation is like confirmation and is done by anointing a person with specially prepared holy oil.) No, infants do not understand what happens in the holy mystery of the Eucharist, but neither do they have to know about the nutritional benefits of mother's milk in order to profit from nursing. We want to provide our children all the spiritual nourishment we can. And truth be told, just how bread and wine become the Body and Blood of the Son of God is beyond the intellectual understanding of even PhD's in theology.

My United Methodist students, as well as those from other denominations that practice "open communion," are often scandalized when they learn that only members of the Orthodox Church may receive this sacrament. They are sometimes at least open to appreciating a different point of view when I tell them that to receive communion in the Orthodox Church is to be in communion with that Church. It is to publicly affirm that one is a fully integrated member of the Body who believes, worships, and lives according to its teachings. In the Eastern Church, Communion has never been a means of evangelism or a tool of ecumenism. Instead, it is the most brilliant icon of the shared life and faith of the Church. Taking Holy Communion is the most intimate participation in the mystery of our salvation possible for a human being. In ancient times, catechumens knew nothing of the Eucharist—and surely had not been present for it—until after their baptism.

St. Justin Martyr wrote that Christian practice in the second century was to serve Communion only to those who had been baptized, believed the apostolic faith, and lived as Christ taught.[7] There certainly were heretical groups in early Christianity, such as Gnostics who denied the Lord's full humanity or sexual libertines who thought that he came to save merely our souls, not our bodies. St. Paul had to deal with that problem in 1 Corinthians 6, as there were church members who saw nothing wrong with having sex with prostitutes.

In our contemporary setting, beliefs about virtually every dimension of theology and ethics are up for grabs. Some who call themselves Christians today do not affirm Jesus Christ's divinity or bodily resurrection, while others have rejected the doctrine of the Holy Trinity as so much outmoded dogmatism. Others have abandoned historic Christian teaching on marriage and sexuality to the point of endorsing intercourse between

---

7. Justin Martyr, "The First Apology of Justin, LXVI, as cited in Roberts and Donaldson, *Ante-Nicene Fathers* 1, 185.

unmarried people or same-sex couples.[8] Some have convinced themselves that greed, disregard for the poor, jingoistic nationalism, and the self-righteous condemnation of others are somehow compatible with the way of Christ. Christianity has become so fragmented and watered down in our culture that the generic identification of "Christian" tends to mean whatever we want it to mean.[9]

Those who hold and live out such views are not in a healthy relationship with Christ or his Church. From an Orthodox perspective, there is neither closed nor open communion. There is simply communion in Christ, which we believe the Eastern Church has maintained whole and complete. Everyone is welcome to enter into that communion, the fullness of the Body of Christ, both in the Eucharist and every other dimension of the life of the Church. The Orthodox perspective is that we do those outside of Orthodoxy no favors by serving them Communion as though it did not matter what they believe or how they live. The Church is in a position to help its members prepare to receive the Lord for their salvation, but we obviously cannot be of much assistance in the preparation of those who are not Orthodox. And when large portions of the Christian community do not believe that bread and wine truly become the Lord's Body and Blood in the Eucharist, it would be quite strange for the Eastern Church to encourage them to receive, and thus affirm, that which they do not believe. The last thing we would want would be to encourage others to eat and drink their own condemnation!

The ancient Christian practice was to receive the Eucharist as often as possible. Unfortunately, laziness and a misinterpretation of what it means to show respect for the sacrament have led many Orthodox to take communion only a few times a year. Fortunately, there is a trend now toward frequent Communion and many people receive the Eucharist weekly. But in any parish, there will be a number of parishioners who do not take Communion on a given day, often for legitimate reasons such as a lack of preparation. This means that non-Orthodox visitors will not stand out by virtue of refraining from Communion. Everyone, Orthodox or not, is invited to come forward at the conclusion of the Liturgy to receive a piece of *antidoron*—which is blessed bread, but not communion—as a sign of hospitality

---

8. For Orthodox statements on same-sex unions, see Hopko, *Christian Faith and Same-Sex Attraction* and LeMasters, *Toward a Eucharistic Vision of Church, Family, Marriage, and Sex*, ch. 6.

9. Douthat, *Bad Religion*, provides an excellent critique of popular Christianity in contemporary America.

and God's blessing. In some ways, offering all present the *antidoron* is similar to "open communion" in churches that have a purely symbolic view of the Lord's Supper, for neither practice involves taking the true Body of Christ.

Conversely, members of the Orthodox Church should not take sacraments in other churches, as doing so would indicate a full agreement with and participation in the faith and life of those communities. So when I attend Methodist chapel services at McMurry, I do not go forward when it is time for communion. (No one seems to notice or be bothered much by that.) Neither do I commune when attending the weddings or ordinations in other churches of family members, friends, and students. On the one hand, the fact that we are not all united in one Eucharist is a sad reminder of the brokenness and division in the Christian community. On the other hand, I do not really want to commune outside the Orthodox Church because of the lack of full agreement about the Christian faith and life among the different denominations.

My students and mainline Protestant friends sometimes object that not sharing Communion with other Christians sends the message that only members of our own church will be saved. Having grown up Southern Baptist, I know that the question of salvation drives most theological discourse in evangelical settings. From an Orthodox perspective, however, things look very different. Eternal judgment is God's business and he alone knows our hearts. *That is not the issue at all when it comes to Communion.*

It sounds really harsh, but I would not serve my own mother Communion as she is a Baptist and consequently does not affirm or participate in the fullness of Orthodox faith and practice. She probably does not want to take Communion in our church as it is her practice to take the Lord's Supper in her own congregation. But as best anyone can tell, Mom embodies personally the virtues and characteristics of a faithful Christian much better than does her youngest son. (Paige agrees heartily with this assessment!) No one can say that Jesus is Lord except by the power of the Holy Spirit (1 Cor 12:3). The prayer used to begin almost all Orthodox services addresses the Holy Spirit as "the Lord and Giver of Life Who art everywhere present and fillest all things." We may put no limits on how the Lord is at work in the lives of other people, regardless of where or even whether they go to church. That is simply not our business. Policies about who can receive the sacraments are not intended to divide eternally the sheep from the goats.

Why, then, is it so important that only Orthodox commune in the Orthodox Church? One point to keep in mind is that sacraments are communal, not individualistic. They are ministries of the Body to heal, strengthen, and bless its various members as they grow in holiness and union with God. We do not receive the sacraments as isolated individuals, but as persons in communion with a visible Body, sharing a common faith and way of life. Those who wish to take Communion in the Church may do so by entering into the communion of the Church, by embracing the fullness of the Orthodox faith. The Church is the Body of Christ and the Eucharist is also his Body and Blood. To ask for the sacrament apart from the Church is to separate Christ from himself and to fail to see that the entire Christian life is sacramental in the sense of being a participation in the holy mystery of our salvation.

The practice of "open communion" threatens to bring about a lowest common denominator attitude toward Christianity that severely challenges the ability of a church to make substantive theological and moral claims to which its members are held accountable. If it is not clear where you are going and the path you are taking to get there, there is not much chance of success. In contrast to minimalistic Christianity, Orthodoxy is maximalist, which means that we want it all. Remember that the goal is to become a partaker of the divine nature, to shine with light as we share in the life of the Holy Trinity (2 Pet 1:4). Eucharistic fellowship is not a bare recognition that those who commune with us at least have warm feelings about Jesus Christ or believe at least a portion of the Nicene Creed. Instead, it is a true participation in the Risen Lord and the glory of his Kingdom. A faith focused on *theosis* tends toward embracing the fullness, not trying to figure out how little one can do and still be saved. Again, that is God's business, not ours.[10]

In some ways, marriage is a good example of what communion with the Lord and his Church means. That should not be surprising since St. Paul spoke of the relationship between husband and wife as a sign of the relationship between Christ and the Church (Eph 5:32). A particular man is married to a particular woman. They are united body and soul in the most intimate ways possible for human beings. They are truly in communion with one another and usually have children who are unique blends of their genetic ancestry, personalities, and habits. Marital union is personal and distinctive; no one marries the general institution of marriage,

---

10. See Alfeyev, *The Mystery of Faith*, 120–29, for a treatment of the relationship between Orthodoxy and other forms of Christianity.

but a particular person with whom they become one flesh. Spouses are not interchangeable.

Likewise, Eastern Christians have unique beliefs and practices which they do not believe are simply one flavor of a larger, less distinctive faith. Instead, they see the fullness of Christianity in the worship, beliefs, iconography, music, and other traditions of the Church that have been kept alive throughout the centuries by the power of the Holy Spirit. They are married to this faith and to the Lord whom they know through it. There is always room for new members of this family, but those new additions must embrace the ongoing experience that is the Orthodox Church. (Remember that the word "orthodox" means both "right worship" and "right belief.") Something like marriage—full, unreserved union with and participation in the Body—is the only kind of Communion that Orthodoxy knows. So at the end of the day, there is neither "open" nor "closed" communion, but simply true Communion with the Lord and his Church.[11]

Back to sports. It is interesting that many people in our culture take athletic teams—and the kind of communion they create between coaches, players, and fans—much more seriously than they do church. Surely, more kids miss church for sports than miss sports for religious activities. Out here in West Texas, it is perfectly normal for teenagers to practice football and other sports in temperatures exceeding 100 degrees for several hours a day every August. Anyone who wants to make a competitive team during the school year had better spend most of the summer in daily workouts and special sports camps, whether or not they are officially required by the coaches. We routinely accept the substantial investments of time, energy, and money that we make in sports, as well as the risks to the health and well being of our children that violent sports like football—and any sports in extreme heat—present. And I know from recruiting honors students for my university that a $500 athletic scholarship often carries more weight in the minds of students and their parents than does a $5,000 academic scholarship. Athletics is *real* and really important in our culture in ways that religion and academics often are not. It is very difficult for many athletes at the end of high school or college to accept that their sports careers are over, even when there is no realistic prospect of moving on to the next level of competition.

---

11. See LeMasters, *Toward a Eucharistic Vision of Church, Family, Marriage, and Sex*, chs. 3–5, for discussions of the relationships between Orthodox views of Communion, the Church, penitential discipline, and marriage.

Perhaps there is something in us that respects demanding endeavors that require a great deal physically and that bring a certain measure of risk. The early Christian writer Tertullian taught that the blood of martyred Christians is the seed of the Church.[12] People were strangely drawn to Christianity by the witness of the martyrs. Something worth dying for must be important, must be worth investigating further. I hear that the Marines are the only branch of the American military service that never has trouble meeting their recruiting quotas. Their boot camp is reportedly the toughest and they have recruiting slogans like "The Few. The Proud. The Marines." Likewise, college students are more likely to join fraternities and sororities, with their demanding and sometimes demeaning expectations for pledging, than literary societies or chess clubs that take membership less seriously. Even the average garage band expects its members to show up for practice and whenever they have a gig.

Again, there is some parallel here to Eastern Christianity. We stand a lot in worship, expect members to pray and fast in a disciplined ways, and require a lengthy period of instruction and formation before one becomes a member of the Church. We use the body in worship by making the sign of the cross, bowing low to make prostrations, and kissing the cross and the icons. Barring extraordinary circumstances, faithful Orthodox believers attend the Divine Liturgy on Sundays and major feast days.

It is not easy to be Orthodox in a conscientious way, but since when was Christianity supposed to be easy? The Lord called his disciples to take up their crosses and follow him, to lose their lives in order to save them, and actually to do the will of his Father in heaven. It is human nature to sacrifice for that which we value, for that which we believe to be of greatest importance. There is no shortage of people willing to lay it all on the line for athletics, whether for themselves or their children. Eastern Christianity reminds us that we should take our faith even more seriously.

Since I make my living as a college professor and am used to the rarified environment of academic life, I was surprised a few years ago to hear a colleague say that student-athletes are usually more influenced by their coaches than by their professors. That makes sense, however, when we think about how much time players spend with coaches, how they learn to follow their instructions with few questions, and how they are part of a cohesive group pursuing a common goal that requires a lot of discipline. Most

---

12. Tertullian, "Apology," L, as cited in Roberts and Donaldson, *The Ante-Nicene Fathers* 3, 55.

coaches whom I have known have a "my way or the highway" approach to their athletes. The same is true of band, choir, and orchestra directors. They know what they want and expect those who sign up to play for them to get with the program.

Though Orthodox bishops and priests do not ask their parishioners to run laps or do push-ups, they do have an authority as spiritual fathers beyond anything I had experienced in other denominations. They are not employees chosen by the congregation and fired at whim, but pastors sent to lead, teach, and console the people under the authority of the bishop, who is the chief pastor of every parish in the diocese. They are always men under authority, priests being responsible to a bishop and bishops being responsible to a more senior bishop or a synod of bishops. Though the canons of the Church are applied pastorally for the salvation of particular people, there is no question that a priest will teach his people to fast, pray, give alms, and go to Confession during Lent, for example. Services will at times be very long. Sermons and classes will address topics that are uncomfortable in contemporary culture. People really are expected to pray and read the Bible daily and to follow the pastoral guidance of their priest.

That is another way of saying we all need coaches and teammates in the Christian life. Someone needs to show us the way and to model what we are being asked to do. Having fellow parishioners seeking to do the same thing is crucial, for few of us really want to be loners. As well, we learn so much from other laypeople as we rear our kids, juggle church and our other commitments and activities, and figure out how to interpret fasting guidelines from antiquity in a fast-food culture. There is a lot of practical activity to undertake and attempt to master in Eastern Christianity. People who like a challenge usually like our Church. Our parish has more converts with martial arts training or military service in their background that one would expect. Both those endeavors require substantial discipline and learning by doing.

Before becoming Orthodox, I participated mostly in churches that did not expect very much of their members. I usually felt that I had to supplement what my congregation or pastor was asking me to do because they were asking so little. I have lived my entire life in one area or another of the Bible Belt and as a Protestant often gravitated toward congregations that defined themselves over against anti-intellectual fundamentalism. (I'm a professor, so what else would you expect?) Granted, it is good not to be an anti-intellectual fundamentalist, but it is even worse to become a knee-jerk reactionary against everything associated with traditional Christianity. I learned over the years that an anti-fundamentalist agenda often throws the baby out with the bathwater and makes it very difficult to grow in the Christian life. It is like the old joke about what you get when you cross a Unitarian with a Jehovah's Witness: Someone who goes around knocking on doors but does not know why. Those without a clear goal hardly ever reach it.

Many people do know what they want, but often it is not to participate by grace in the divine nature, as that sounds highly inconvenient (2 Pet 1:4). They may want an inspiring sermon, a vibrant youth group for their kids, very few demands on their time and energy, and as little theology as possible. A religion that fits comfortably into a middle-class lifestyle without claiming much of our time and energy—or calling for personal transformation—remains quite popular in American culture. Whether it is the "wealth and success gospel" or some version of the social gospel, it is usually more popular to fit God into our agendas than for us to allow our plans to be questioned by his. Regardless of whether they are called liberal or conservative, such approaches have trouble helping people grow in holiness because Christ's Kingdom is not simply life as usual with good feelings about Jesus. He calls us to take up our crosses, die to self, and shine with light. I do not know about you, but I need to get to work in order to have any chance of doing that.

Eastern Christianity is not shy about telling people that we actually need to do something—yes, to work—in order to become participants in the divine nature. Whereas in the past I had to add to what churches expected of me in order to be stretched spiritually, now I cannot even begin to keep up. Loving and forgiving enemies, being in constant prayer, fighting self-centered passions, for example, are tough challenges. It is so tempting to do just about anything other than pray and to find some way to overindulge while keeping the letter, but not the spirit, of the fasting guidelines of the Church. But even that is fairly small stuff when we remember what *theosis* means: to be united with the Holy Trinity and shine with the divine glory like an iron left in the fire. I have no illusions that I am anywhere near that goal.

My Protestant friends now probably want to direct me to the writings of Martin Luther and John Calvin. The Protestant Reformation rightly criticized the corrupt approach to "works righteousness" in medieval Roman Catholicism that encouraged people to earn their way into heaven by doing enough good deeds by their own power. Buy enough indulgences, pay for enough masses, visit enough shrines, and you are good to go. The most profound spiritual matters were obscured by a focus on going through the motions and money changing hands.

There was never a need for a reformation in the East, however, because the Orthodox Church did not sell indulgences or otherwise encourage people to think that they could save themselves. Eastern Christianity teaches that salvation is about sharing in the Lord's victory over death and fulfillment of humanity's original calling to become like God in holiness. We obviously cannot do that on our own just by trying really hard. Orthodox saints do not boast of their holiness; in fact, they are totally blind to it. The closer we grow to the Lord, the more aware we are of the infinite journey before us to become perfect as our Father in heaven is perfect. The early Egyptian monk Abba Sisoes was a very righteous man, but when on his death bed he saw the angels coming and asked for more time to repent. "You have no need to do penance, Father," a fellow monk assured him. Sisoes responded, "Truly, I do not think that I have even made a beginning yet."[13]

In contrast, Western Christianity has historically had a more legal orientation focused on meeting God's standards. The debate between faith and works reflects that approach, as the controversy is over how successful we can be in meeting those requirements and how we are made right with God when we fall short. Catholic and Protestant theology both tend to view salvation more as a remedy for sin than as the fulfillment of humanity's original calling to become like God, to become a partaker of the divine nature.

Thankfully, that debate has never been much of an issue in the Eastern Church. As St. James taught in his epistle, "faith without works is dead" (Jas 2:26). Orthodoxy affirms that a person who believes must cooperate with God's grace by living faithfully, rather like how a drowning person will reach out for a lifeline. Only an idiot would take credit for grasping a flotation device thrown to him by a rescuer, but the endangered swimmer still has to do his part to receive help by grabbing and holding on. Mental or spiritual trust in the flotation device alone will not keep him from sinking to the bottom. He has to act accordingly. Of course, Orthodox Christians know that we are saved by God's grace. The Jesus Prayer is at the heart of our spiritual tradition: "Lord Jesus Christ, Son of God, have mercy on me, a

---

13. "Sisoes," as cited in Ward, *The Sayings of the Desert Fathers*, 215.

sinner." But we still have to open our lives to the Lord's mercy, to crucify the self-centered desires to which we have become enslaved. As St. Paul wrote, "work out your own salvation with fear and trembling; for God is at work in you..." (Phil 2:12–13). Otherwise, we risk becoming like those who say "Lord, Lord" but do not do the will of the Father. Then Christ will say that He never knew us (Matt 7:21–23).

The parable of the Last Judgment in Matthew 25 is a powerful example of how our actions are icons of our relationship with Christ. In that account, those who cared for the hungry, thirsty, naked, sick, and imprisoned actually cared for the Lord. Those who did not disregarded him. The eternal judgment of the sheep and goats reflected what they did in relation to their needy neighbors. If we say that we love God and hate our brothers and sisters, we are liars (1 John 4:20). Conversely, if we love and serve those who bear God's image, we love and serve him. The point is not that we earn salvation by doing a lot of social work. It is, instead, that that those who are in Christ will take on his qualities and shine brightly with his light and love. This is *theosis* in action. If we have received Christ's love and mercy, we must show that grace to others. If we refuse to do so, we reject the Lord and obviously do not share in his holiness.

As a Texan, I have to direct us back to sports yet again. Can you imagine members of an athletic team without a shared goal of actually playing their particular sport as best they could? How successful would coaches be who limited the required drills and practice schedule for fear that the players would place more emphasis on working hard than on trusting the good will of the coaches? The parallels are not exact, but the point is clear. There is no necessary contradiction between giving due attention to both God's mercy and how we live. The worship and spiritual disciplines of Orthodoxy do require a lot effort; they are a form of work. But they are not vain human efforts to impress God or earn our way into his life. Instead, they are blessed paths that the Lord has given us for the healing of our souls and bodies. The Holy Spirit calls us to take these paths of worship, prayer, fasting, confession, almsgiving, forgiveness, reconciliation, etc., in ways that calm our inflamed passions and bring us more fully into union with God. We are called to become *participants* in the divine nature. Participation is active, not passive. It requires something of us.

Athletes and their fans know that there is nothing like an actual game to express their collective purpose and identity. Not many show up to watch practices, but the stands are often filled for an anticipated contest between cross town rivals, like Abilene High and Abilene Cooper. A team member or a fan who does not show up for big games is hardly a member of the community. Likewise, in early Christianity a believer who did not come to worship for three consecutive Sundays was presumed to be dead, seriously ill, or to have abandoned the faith. Orthodox Christians are expected to attend the Divine Liturgy every Sunday and on major feast days, which fall throughout the week at various times of year. Of course, there will be times when someone is sick, has to work or go to school, or is otherwise "providentially hindered" as I remember a Baptist pastor saying years ago. But otherwise, believers should be at church to pray, even when we are visiting another town or have guests visiting us. Though the Eastern Church does not have the Roman Catholic concept of a "holy day of obligation," regular attendance at Liturgy is a basic and expected spiritual discipline. The scriptures warn against forsaking the assembly (Heb 10:25) and Acts describes the Lord's followers meeting on Sunday to pray and celebrate Communion (Acts 20:7). Orthodoxy follows that pattern to this day.

The worship of the Eastern Church embodies and enacts our salvation in Jesus Christ. We join with other members of the Body to offer our prayer and praise to God. We hear the scriptures, receive instruction, and offer bread and wine for the miracle of the Eucharist. Communicants are nourished by the Body and Blood of Christ and truly participate in the Wedding Feast of the Lamb. The work of the people in the worship of God on Sunday prepares Orthodox believers to offer their lives to God the rest of the week, to live each day in communion with Christ. Like the bread and wine, people are not ends in themselves; but when offered to the Holy Trinity, they are transformed by divine glory. Those who take Christ into their own lives in Communion are called to make every dimension of their presence in the world a Eucharist, a participation in the blessed life of the eternal Kingdom.

Two processions during every Divine Liturgy are known as entrances.[14] During one, the priest or deacon carries the book containing the Gospel readings from the altar to the nave (where the congregants are) and then back into the altar area. This entrance represents Christ's Incarnation, as he comes down from heaven to earth. The second entrance, during which the priest and deacon carry the bread and wine for the Eucharist into the altar, represents Christ's journey to the cross where he offers himself in free obedience to the Holy Trinity. Those who participate in the Divine Liturgy are

---

14. See Farley, *Let Us Attend,* for an excellent commentary on the different dimensions of the Divine Liturgy.

to live it out every day of their lives. The entire Christian life is an entrance with the Lord into the life of the Kingdom. Orthodox Christians are to live the new life that the Lord's Incarnation has brought to the world each day. We are also to join ourselves to Christ's offering, dying to self as we grow in love and service to him and to all who bear his image and likeness.

So just as athletes have to work out daily, so do we. The most fundamental exercise of the Christian life is prayer, and Orthodox Christians should pray at least once a day in the "icon corner" of their home. That is a place normally with an icon of Jesus Christ, the Virgin Mary, and the patron saints of the members of the household. Orthodox families gather there to have their morning, mid-day, or evening prayers and to read the Bible and accounts of the lives of the saints. Not every Orthodox family does it that way, but it is normal practice in the Church to have such a space set aside for prayer. Of course, God can hear our prayers no matter where we are. But if something is important to us, we give it its own spot with a name, such as dining rooms, bed rooms, living rooms, etc. If we value something, we give it time and attention. What could be more worthy of such regard than praying to God?

If our schedule changes unexpectedly or we are otherwise prevented from keeping our usual rule of prayer, we may say the Jesus Prayer at any point during the day or pray using our own words or those we have memorized from our regular prayers while driving, walking, or sitting in our offices. God is not a stickler who demands that we follow a certain formula in prayer in order for us to be heard.[15] Remember the thief on the cross and the repentant publican in the parable. A few words from the heart are sufficient. The Our Father or the Lord's Prayer is quite short itself and the model prayer for all Christians. The main point is for prayer from the depths of our being to become part of the rhythm of our lives, for an earnest plea from a contrite and humble heart to be at the center of our relationship with the Lord. We are shaped and prepared for that kind of devotion by the corporate prayer life of the Church in the Divine Liturgy, Vespers, Matins, the Hours, and the other liturgical services. The forms used by Orthodox laypeople in their daily prayers are often abbreviated versions of those services. Even when we pray by ourselves, we are not praying alone, but also with the Church and the entire heavenly host.

Anyone may shoot baskets, play catch, or swing a club or a bat. They may not be on a team or engaged in their sport in any formal capacity, but

---

15. See Theophan the Recluse, *The Spiritual Life*, 204ff.

what they do is still dependent upon the tradition of an organized athletic activity, of an ongoing community much larger than themselves. Baseball is older than a kindergartner throwing a ball to his dad. The same is true whenever we say the Lord's Prayer, the Jesus Prayer, one of the Psalms, or chant a hymn from a service. Regardless of whether we are in a church building, we pray as members of Christ's Body in communion with other Orthodox around the world and those who have gone on to be in the presence of the Lord.

To participate in this team is a far more profound undertaking than being in any athletic organization. While there are many parallels between Orthodox Christianity and sports, there is no comparison between sharing in the eternal life of the Holy Trinity and winning even a world championship in any league. At the end of the day, sport is about the glory of human accomplishment; it obviously cannot conquer death or make us holy. Nonetheless, it is instructive to keep the parallels in mind because God's salvation is the fulfillment of our humanity. It is not surprising that some of the same dynamics we encounter in the Christian life are also present in other activities toward which human beings are naturally inclined. The Lord does not ask us to abandon our humanity, but to become fully human in his image and likeness. He asks us to leave behind only that which makes us less, not more, the people we were created to be. The dimensions of athletics that people and cultures across the world find so attractive point us to the discipline, community, and worship of a Kingdom that is not of this world. If players and fans will accept such hardships for the passing glory of sports, shouldn't we be willing to sacrifice infinitely more to become partakers of the divine nature? Eastern Christianity certainly thinks so.

5

FOOLS, MONKS, AND MARTYRS

DULL. BORING. CONVENTIONAL. THESE words describe the reputation that Christians often have as members of the most popular religion in American society. There are exceptions that prove the rule, but we rarely encounter Christianity actually tottering on the edge of social respectability or shocking anyone. Instead, believers often act, speak, and think in ways that obscure the contrast between the Kingdom of God and the kingdoms of this world by watering down the faith to a bit of religious icing on a cake of mainstream life. Comfort, convenience, and status then take precedence over God in our list of priorities. Christians become indistinguishable from everyone else in how they live. At that point, we are definitely not the salt of the earth.

The Orthodox Church is very different in this respect because many of its great saints looked like nuts—or worse—from the perspective of the dominant cultures of their day. They were not normal in the sense of following what was popular, easy, and helped them get ahead. Instead, they challenged common assumptions about what it means to live as a Christian and refused to let anyone identify God's reign with business as usual in our corrupt world. That is true of the ancient and current witness of martyrs who accept torture and death before abandoning their faith.[1]

The first extended account of martyrdom that we have from the early church is that of St. Polycarp in the mid-second century. As Polycarp stood before an angry pagan crowd in a stadium, the Roman official urged him

---

1. This chapter draws on material also presented in an article that I have co-authored with John-Eric Swenson, "St. Symeon, Fool for Christ and Exemplar of Humility," *The American Benedictine Review* 64:3 (September 2013): 267–81.

to "Respect your age," take an oath in Caesar's name, "change your mind, [and] say 'Away with the atheists!'" (Since the Christians would not worship the Roman gods, the pagans charged them with atheism.) Instead of doing the apparently sensible thing and saving his life, the elderly bishop "looked sternly at the whole crowd . . . indicating them with a wave of the hand . . . and said, 'Away with the atheists!'" In response to the promise that he would be set free if he would take a simple pagan oath, the old saint said of Jesus Christ, "I have served him eighty-six years and in no way has he dealt unjustly with me; so how can I blaspheme my king who saved me?"[2] By the conventional standards of that society, Polycarp was a fool who needlessly suffered execution due to his obsession with a fantasy.

The same is also true of monks and nuns who forgo marriage, family, money, normal clothing, and much else in order to devote themselves to prayer, obedience, and other spiritual disciplines in monastic communities. St. Antony the Great lived from the mid-third to the mid-fourth century and was one of the first Christian monks in the Egyptian desert. When Antony heard Jesus Christ's words to the rich young ruler read in church, "If you would be perfect, go, sell what you possess and give to the poor, and you will have treasure in heaven" (Matt 19:21), he took this instruction as a personal command from the Lord. He then began a life of severe asceticism in the desert, including living alone in a tomb with hardly any food as a hermit for years. During this time, the demons beat him physically, appeared as wild beasts and in other terrifying forms, and tempted him in every way imaginable.[3] He emerged from these ordeals in perfect health and peace, and taught those who came to him for guidance with great wisdom. Many joined him in the monastic life and everyone who came to Antony for guidance was blessed for growth as a Christian.

Of course, people who abandon a conventional life for prayer, fasting, and spiritual struggle in the desert probably looked no less crazy in the fourth century than they do to many people today. Protestants especially have little appreciation for monasticism, as their churches rejected the institution at the time of the Reformation. Vows of celibacy may seem contradictory to the blessed state of marriage or even to our nature as man and woman; keep in mind, however, that Jesus Christ, John the Baptist, and the prophet Elijah never married. St. Paul was probably a widower and saw spiritual advantages to being unmarried: "The unmarried man is anxious

---

2. "The Martyrdom of Polycarp," VIII/9, as cited in Sparks, *The Apostolic Fathers*, 143.
3. Athanasius, *The Life of Antony and The Letter to Marcellinus*, 31–42.

about the affairs of the Lord, how to please the Lord; but the married man is anxious about worldly affairs, how to please his wife, and his interests are divided" (1 Cor 7:32–34). Without denying the great blessings of marriage, Eastern Christianity recognizes that God calls people to different styles of life and to different ministries. After forbidding divorce except in cases of infidelity, the Lord responded to the disciples' comment that "If such is the case of a man with his wife, it is not expedient to marry," with the teaching that "Not all men can receive this saying, but only those to whom it is given. For there are eunuchs who have been so from birth, and there are eunuchs who have been made eunuchs by men, and there are eunuchs who have made themselves eunuchs for the sake of the kingdom of heaven. He who is able to receive this, let him receive it" (Matt 19:10–12).

Of course, Christ was not recommending physical castration. To become a eunuch for the heavenly kingdom in this sense means to forgo marriage and sexual intimacy for the sake of responding to a different calling, as there are types of ministry more compatible with singleness than with marriage. For example, people who follow literally the Lord's instruction to sell their possessions, give the proceeds to the poor, and to follow him, probably should not get married and rear children. They may be able to minister to residents of a homeless shelter or halfway house by actually sharing the day-to-day challenges of those who have virtually nothing in this world. Missionaries in war-torn or developing nations may find that the freedom and flexibility of the celibate life enables them to take the risks that are necessary to show Christ's love to people who live in such circumstances.

In the Orthodox Church, God calls some men and women to lifelong celibacy in religious communities that become like new families to them. The monks and nuns do not have private property and work to support the community through which their material needs are met. Their daily schedules revolve around prayer; laypeople come to them for spiritual guidance. Monasteries are like retreat centers where everyone is welcome to benefit from the wisdom of believers so committed to the Lord that they give up all semblance of a conventional life in order to devote themselves to spiritual struggle and prayer. It takes years of spiritual formation before someone may be tonsured as a monk or nun with a lifelong commitment to this way of life. The Church forces no one to become a monastic and certainly does not believe that monks and nuns are necessarily holier than married people. They hear a different calling, however, and make a bold witness in stark contrast to a culture that prizes money, sex, and power above all else.

From the perspective of that culture, they—like the martyrs—are surely religious fanatics who have needlessly deprived themselves of the good life. But for Eastern Christians, these brothers and sisters in black robes are reminders that God's Kingdom is not of this world.

In the spirituality of the Eastern Church, there is an even more curious figure called "a fool for Christ." In order to grasp his or her importance, it helps to remember the example of major biblical prophets who exhibited behaviors that made them appear foolish, if not mentally ill, to their contemporaries. God commanded Isaiah to go naked and barefoot (Isa 20:2–3), while Ezekiel was to lie on his left side for over a year and to cook his food over a fire fueled by dung (Ezek 4:1–15). God had Hosea marry a prostitute (Hos 3:1–3), and John the Baptist subsisted on locusts and honey while living in the desert (Matt 3:4). These actions put them well outside of conventional modes of behavior. Likewise, St. Paul called the cross of Christ "foolishness" to the Greeks and reminded the Corinthians that "God has chosen the foolish things of the world to put to shame the wise . . . " (1 Cor 1:23, 27). The very "message of the cross is foolishness to those who are perishing, but to those who are being saved it is the power of God" (1 Cor 1:18). And as St. Paul says of his own ministry, "We are fools for Christ's sake . . . " (1 Cor 4:10).

It is easy to forget that some of Jesus Christ's own family members apparently thought that he had lost his mind (Mark 3:21). He turned over the tables of the moneychangers in the Temple, publically violated Sabbath rules, and associated with Gentiles and sinners in ways that were unthinkable—and quite dangerous—for a Jewish Messiah. By refusing political power and accepting crucifixion, he acted in ways that seemed totally crazy. That is still how we often view people who wind up dying for their beliefs when they could have lived by compromising just a bit.

The root meaning of the word "saint" is "holy," and the Orthodox Church has recognized as saints several people whose lives were characterized by displays of bizarre behavior that made them appear insane or even irreligious and immoral. However, the Church remembers these holy fools as people of sound mind and great holiness. They chose to manifest apparent mental illness in order to embrace Christ-like humility, to minister to those on the margins of society, and to make a prophetic witness against corruption in both the Church and the larger culture. They sought to embody the foolishness of the gospel in their own lives.

This kind of folly serves no practical purpose, but instead intends to shock people as the fool prophetically awakens others from their self-satisfied delusions and calls them to repentance. For example, the fool for Christ Nicolas of Pskov handed Tsar Ivan the Terrible a bloody piece of meat, which he refused on the grounds that eating meat violated the Lenten fast.[4] St. Nicolas replied, "And . . . it is unlawful to eat a piece of beast's flesh in Lent and not to eat up so much man's flesh as he hath done already?" This prophetic word persuaded Ivan to stop the looting of the city of Pskov.[5] Only someone respected as a holy fool could have gotten away with speaking like that to a bloodthirsty tyrant.

St. Isidora may be the first of this type of saint in the history of the Church; she lived in an Egyptian woman's monastery in the late fourth century. "Feigning madness, she worked in the kitchen, with rags wrapped round her head instead of the monastic cowl. She undertook all the most menial tasks and was treated with general contempt, kicked and insulted by the other nuns." When the spiritual insight of a visiting revered ascetic revealed that this woman was a very holy person, she actually ran away in order to avoid the praise of others.[6] Some fools for Christ were monks who refused to defend themselves even against paternity charges, their innocence being revealed only later through unanticipated circumstances.[7] In the sixth century, the youths Theophilus and Maria scandalized respectable people by presenting themselves as a jester and a prostitute as they wandered the streets of Antioch. They did so because they wanted to become humble by enduring contempt and thus getting over their obsession with their egos.[8]

As strange as their behavior seems, the Orthodox Church does not view these saints as victims of pathological self-loathing or of mental disorders. Instead, Eastern Christianity sees them as radical prophets who know that holiness is not the same as social conformity and worldly success. Since all human beings sin, they identified with reprobates and social outcasts in order to show that the universal human condition is one of corruption and weakness, which requires salvation beyond mere good behavior.[9] In contrast to the relatively easy way of social conformity, they took up their crosses, died to illusions of their own virtue, and trusted in God's mercy to save them. What St. Paul wrote of the apostles applies to the holy fools,

---

4. Ware, *The Orthodox Way*, 99.
5. Ware, *The Inner Kingdom*, 177.
6. Ibid., 157.
7. Yannaras, *The Freedom of Morality*, 68.
8. Ibid., 69–70.
9. Ibid., 74.

"To the present hour we hunger and thirst, we are ill-clad and buffeted and homeless ... When reviled, we bless; when persecuted, we endure; when slandered, we try to conciliate; we have become, and are now, as the refuse of the world, the off-scouring of all things" (1 Cor 4:11–13).

Eastern Orthodoxy understands fools for Christ to be people called by God to a unique form of ministry that speaks prophetically both to the church and to the world. They have been most prominent when Christianity is well-established in a society and overly domesticated according to conventional standards. When "people were in danger of confusing an earthly kingdom with the Kingdom of God, then there was an urgent need of the fool's mockery."[10] Since so many Americans assume that being a good Christian simply means being nice, moral, patriotic, and middle class, we could use some holy fools to shock us out of our complacency.

Orthodoxy views salvation as a process of *theosis*, of growth in holiness and union with God as human beings become "partakers of the divine nature" (2 Pet 1:4) in Jesus Christ by the power of the Holy Spirit. The example and teaching of the fools challenge us to participate more fully in the life of Christ. They follow in the way of biblical prophets who said and did unusual things in order to get the attention of their audience and present effectively a message that was often difficult to accept. Like Isaiah, Ezekiel, Hosea, John the Baptist, and even Jesus Christ, they do apparently foolish things in order to speak and enact the word of God.

Though I do not know anyone personally who fits the type perfectly, a few characters have crossed my path who have something of the fool for Christ in them. They are people who have had mental and physical challenges whom it would be easy simply to define by their medical diagnoses. But that would be to miss the point because their lives shine with a simple trust in God that shames my tendency to rely on my own wits, health, and resources. After going on about what is close to nonsense, they sometimes articulate deep spiritual truths clearly. They may live in poverty or in institutionalized settings, but there is sometimes a peace about them and their surroundings that is not of this world. They behave strangely, at times comically, but God is real to them in a way that our adult seriousness easily obscures. No, I do not know quite what to make of these folks, but am glad that I have met them and bow before the mystery of the One whom they serve in such childlike ways. Remember that Jesus Christ said something about becoming a little child in order to enter the heavenly Kingdom (Matt 18:3). Eastern Christianity knows that we will find salvation through

10. Ware, *The Inner Kingdom*, 170.

childlike humility and trust in the Lord, not by appearing wise and powerful in the eyes of the world.

St. Symeon is the best known fool for Christ in Eastern Christianity; his life was recorded by Leontius, Bishop of Neapolis on Cyprus in the seventh century.[11] Though it is impossible to verify the historical accuracy of this account of Symeon's life, the document is "an 'icon' of the holy fool, offering a typical picture of what, in the Orthodox tradition, the holy fool is supposed to be."[12] Let's dig a bit more deeply into Symeon's life.

St. Symeon, who lived during the sixth century, befriended in Jerusalem a young man from Syria named John. After they prayed together for divine guidance, they left for a monastery in the region of the Jordan.[13] They followed in the tradition of monasticism associated with St. Antony the Great of Egypt, of the fourth century, who is often described as the first Christian monk. As mentioned earlier, Antony had given away all his possessions and lived a solitary life in the desert where he engaged in tremendous spiritual warfare in preparation for a ministry of providing guidance and instruction to people of all walks of life who sought him out.[14] Antony is one of the Desert Fathers, the name given to the ascetics who gave up a conventional life in order to find their salvation like St. John the Baptist in the searing heat of the desert.[15]

Leaving behind their family ties, Symeon and John went to a monastery where they were welcomed by a monk named Nikon, a holy man known for signs, wonders, and the gift of prophecy, by which he had anticipated their arrival. Nikon addressed Symeon as a "welcome fool" when he arrived at the monastery and promptly tonsured them as monks. After praying for God's guidance to find a suitable place to live in the desert, they went to a location near the Dead Sea, where Symeon spent the next twenty-nine years living in a cave with John.[16] The pair underwent great spiritual struggles with temptations common to desert ascetics, living lives of extreme physical depravation in the wilderness. They advanced in a few years to the point of receiving visions, revelations, and miracles from God. After he spent twenty-nine years undergoing such trials, Symeon said to John, "What more benefit do we derive, brother, from passing time in this desert?

11. Krueger, *Symeon the Holy Fool.*
12. Ware, *The Inner Kingdom*, 158.
13. Krueger, *Symeon the Holy Fool*, 135.
14 See Athanasius, *Life of Antony and Letter to Marcellinus.*
15. See Ward, *The Sayings of the Desert Fathers* and *The Lives of the Desert Fathers.*
16. Krueger, *Symeon the Holy Fool*, 144.

But if you hear me, get up, let us depart; let us save others. For as we are, we do not benefit anyone except ourselves, and have not brought anyone else to salvation." In response to John's protests, Symeon said, "Believe me, I won't stay, but I will go in the power of Christ; I will mock the world."[17]

Symeon parted from John by leaving the desert in obedience to a divine command to take up this unusual ministry: "Do not fear, brother John; for it is not by my own (will) that I wish to do this, but because God commands me."[18] He went with an evangelistic intention that is common to the fools for Christ. Strengthened by lengthy periods of spiritual and ascetical formation, he was prepared to engage the world by presenting a prophetic message and witness that highlights the irreconcilable tension between God's Kingdom and the ways of the world.[19] Symeon stopped for three days in Jerusalem to pray at various holy sites, where "his every prayer was that his works might be hidden until his departure from life, so that he might escape human glory, through which human arrogance and conceit arises . . ."[20] He wanted to preserve his humility and not to fall prey to pride.

Symeon began his ministry of prophetic folly by dragging a dead dog by his belt as he entered the city of Emesa (the present-day city of Homs in Syria). The very next day, which was a Sunday, he disrupted a church service by throwing nuts at the burning candles; he then ran to the pulpit and threw nuts at women in the congregation. When he was chased out of the church, Symeon turned over tables belonging to pastry chefs (an act reminiscent of Jesus Christ's action against the moneychangers in the courtyard of the Temple). He was nearly beaten to death for this disruptive behavior.[21] No pastor would welcome such behavior in the church, but perhaps these unusual actions were necessary to criticize the complacency of a community at ease with rituals and a lively trade of baked goods, but indifferent to true faith and repentance. The fool "does not mock Holy Scripture or the Creed, the sacraments or the icons. He mocks only the pompous and self-satisfied who hold high office in the Church and the humorless ritualists who confuse outer gesture with inner life."[22]

On some Sundays, Symeon actually wore a string of sausage around his neck like a deacon's stole; he would eat sausages all day, dipping them in

---

17. Ibid., 148.
18. Ibid., 149.
19. Ware, *The Inner Kingdom*, 168.
20. Krueger, *Symeon the Holy Fool*, 150.
21. Ibid., 151.
22. Ware, *The Inner Kingdom*, 169.

mustard from a bucket that he carried.²³ These actions were likely highly offensive to the sensibilities of the established Christian community. Not only did Symeon apparently mock the liturgical attire of deacons, he also substituted gluttonous indulgence in meat for the expected fast in preparation for receiving communion. Such actions certainly did not give the impression of being a faithful Christian, especially for one dressed as a monk. Yet when a man with diseased eyes ridiculed him, Symeon rubbed them with the mustard, which caused great pain. After disregarding Symeon's instructions to wash in garlic and vinegar, the man went to a doctor and became totally blind. He finally obeyed Symeon's instructions, was healed, and thanked God. Then Symeon exclaimed, "Never again steal your neighbor's goats."²⁴ God worked through his outlandish display to restore the man's sight and call him to repentance.

After having fasted completely for a week, Symeon worked briefly for a soup merchant, but was beaten and fired when he gorged himself on the soup and gave the rest away. Symeon later miraculously burned incense in his hand and on his cloak without them catching fire. Through this and later encounters with him, the merchant and his wife left a heretical sect for the communion of the Orthodox Church. Symeon left that neighborhood "until the deed which he had done was forgotten. He hurried on immediately elsewhere to do something inappropriate, so that he might thereby hide his perfection."²⁵

Symeon's holiness was then recognized by the proprietor of a tavern, where he destroyed a container of wine that had been poisoned by a snake. In order to avoid praise, he pretended to disrobe in the bedroom of the man's wife who thought that Symeon wanted to rape her; again, he was beaten and treated with contempt. The proprietor refused the suggestion that Symeon merely feigned bad character, noting that the monk routinely ate meat in violation of the fasting practices expected of monastics and, on fasting days and seasons, of all Orthodox Christians. Leontius writes that "without tasting bread all week, the righteous one often ate meat. No one knew about his fasting, since he ate meat in front of everybody in order to deceive them."²⁶ Indeed, Symeon would not eat at all from the beginning of Lent until Thursday of Holy Week—a very long total fast. On one such occasion, he spent the morning of Holy Thursday in a cake shop, stuffing

23. Krueger, *Symeon the Holy Fool*, 164.
24. Ibid.
25. Ibid., 152, 158.
26. Ibid., 153.

himself in order to give the impression that he was a glutton who did not fast at all.[27]

This kind of deception is characteristic of the fools for Christ, who wish to keep their sanctity and sanity a secret. Symeon also relieved himself in public without shame out of a desire to make everyone think that he was out of his mind.[28] At times, "he dragged himself along on his buttocks," deliberately tripped people who were running, babbled, and rolled on the ground when there was a new moon.[29] He apparently took every opportunity to make others think that he was crazy, and revealed his sanity to Deacon John alone, a friend who is not to be confused with Symeon's earlier companion of the same name.

On one occasion, after eating nothing throughout the season of Lent, Symeon was so weak that Deacon John suggested that he bathe. Symeon agreed, but then stripped off his clothes in public and tied them like a turban around his head. He then entered the women's section of the bathhouse, where the women beat him and threw him out. In response to the deacon's question about how he felt in the women's bath, Symeon said that he had no sexual thoughts at all: "the whole of my mind was on God's work, and I did not part from Him."[30]

This description reflects Symeon's attainment of a state of freedom from passions such as lust. In Eastern Christian tradition, prayer, fasting, and other forms of asceticism are tools for gaining control over disordered desires; they provide strength in rejecting self-centered attachments and redirecting our desires to God. In this sense, Symeon "possessed *apatheia* or dispassion—purity of the passions, inner freedom, integration and integrity of both soul and body."[31] Symeon lived in complete poverty and devoted his nights to prayer, not sleep.[32] His severe self-denial enabled him to experience no sexual urges even in the presence of naked women. In fact, instances of nakedness are not uncommon among fools for Christ. Their nakedness reminds us of "the innocence of Adam in Paradise before the fall, when he was naked and unashamed."[33] Symeon displayed such purity by remaining free from lust even as he frolicked with "disreputable women

27. Ibid., 160.
28. Ibid., 153.
29. Ibid., 159.
30. Ibid., 154.
31. Ware, *The Inner Kingdom*, 166.
32. Krueger, *Symeon the Holy Fool*, 168.
33. Ware, *The Inner Kingdom*, 155.

(who) threw their hands into his lap, fondled him, poked him, and pinched him . . . " God miraculously gave him money which he used to pay prostitutes to become his faithful "girlfriends," which entailed a commitment to chastity.[34]

Symeon did not defend himself when wrongly accused of raping and impregnating a slave girl, even referring to the unborn child as "a little Symeon" and saying "Eat, my wife" to the girl as he brought her nourishing food during the pregnancy. After struggling to deliver the child for three days and almost dying, the young woman confessed that Symeon was not the father.[35] By accepting and even seeking the contempt of others, Symeon intended to grow in humility.[36] Eastern Orthodox spiritual tradition understands the acceptance of false judgment as a sign of victory over the vices of pride and vainglory. St. Issac the Syrian wrote, "A man who is truly humble is not troubled when he is wronged, and he says nothing to justify himself against the injustice, but he accepts slander as truth; he does not attempt to persuade men that he is calumniated, but he begs forgiveness."[37] Indeed, those who wrongly condemn the innocent are to be welcomed as physicians for the soul as they aid in the attainment of humility.

Symeon behaved in outrageous, scandalous ways that gave others the impression that he was insane or demon-possessed and anything but a righteous person. Nonetheless, God healed the sick, cast out demons, and called many people to faith and repentance through his ministry. His marginal social and religious status apparently made it possible for him to engage people in unique ways, especially people who would likely not have been receptive to a more conventional evangelist. Jesus Christ's shocking association with tax collectors and prostitutes made it possible for such despised persons to respond to his ministry. Likewise, Symeon's embrace of a very low social standing enabled those normally estranged from dominant social institutions, including the Church, to recognize him as one of their own. Perhaps because he made himself lower than others, people let down their resistance to his message.

The example of St. Symeon as a fool for Christ was shocking to his contemporaries and may appear truly bizarre to contemporary Christians who have probably never considered feigned mental illness a legitimate, or

34. Krueger, *Symeon the Holy Fool*, 159.

35. Ibid., 156.

36. Larchet, *Mental Disorders and Spiritual Healing*, 140.

37. Issac the Syrian, *Ascetical Homilies*, 6, as cited in Larchet, *Mental Disorders and Spiritual Healing*, 141.

even plausible, form of witness or ministry. One way to appreciate Symeon, and to learn from his unusual example, concerns his radical exemplification of the virtue of humility, which is the opposite of the primordial and deadly sin of pride. Orthodox spiritual teaching maintains that "humility should be the first concern of those who are fighting the presumption of the devil, for as we advance it will be a sure guide to all the paths of virtue."[38] Christians of whatever epoch or denominational identity should be able to gain important insights about this central characteristic of discipleship from Symeon the fool for Christ.

Recall that Symeon was prepared to play the fool by decades of spiritual struggle as a monastic in the desert. He was strengthened by a tradition of spiritual formation that highly prized humility as a necessary quality for the Christian life, and especially for those who abandoned the world in order to devote themselves to prayer, poverty, chastity, and obedience. A story about the fourth-century desert father Macarius the Great illumines the fundamental role of humility for monks and nuns:

> When Abba Macarius was returning from the marsh to his cell one day carrying some palm-leaves, he met the devil on the road with a scythe. The latter struck at him as much as he pleased, but in vain, and he said to him, "What is your power, Macarius, that makes me powerless against you? All that you do, I do, too; you fast, so do I; you keep vigil, and I do not sleep at all; in one thing only do you beat me." Abba Macarius asked what that was. He said, "Your humility. Because of that I can do nothing against you."[39]

A similar account comes from the nun Amma Theodora, who reported that

> There was a hermit who was able to banish the demons. And he asked them: "What makes you go away? Is it fasting?" They replied: "We do not eat or drink." "Is it vigils?" They said: "We do not sleep." "Then what power sends you away?" They replied: "Nothing can overcome us except humility alone." Amma Theodora said: "Do you see how humility is victorious over the demons?"[40]

By acting in ways that gave the impression that he was insane, immoral, and irreligious,

---

38. Diadochos of Photiki, "On Spiritual Knowledge and Discrimination," as cited in Palmer, *The Philokalia* 1, 265.

39. Abba Macarius, as quoted in Ward, *The Sayings of the Desert Fathers*, 129–30.

40. Amma Theodora, as quoted in Chryssavgis, *In the Heart of the Desert*, 73.

Symeon sought to embrace, as fully as humanly possible, the virtue necessary for victory over the corrupting powers of sin and evil in his own life. St. Hesychios the Priest notes that humility "destroys in us all that is evil and hateful" and is consequently "difficult to attain." "Even if you can easily find someone who . . . practices a number of virtues, you will hardly find the odor of humility in him . . . It is something that can be acquired only with much diligence."[41] Given the difficulty of becoming humble, it is not surprising that Symeon went to great lengths to acquire this elusive trait of soul. The comments of St. Diadochos of Photiki about a humble priest apply also to what Symeon sought to achieve: "In his extreme love for God, he strips himself of any thought of his own dignity; and with a spirit of humility he buries in the depths of divine love any pride to which his high position might give rise . . . We too should do the same, fleeing all honor and glory in the overwhelming richness of our love for the Lord who loves us so greatly."[42]

Jesus Christ taught and embodied humility throughout his ministry, reserving his strongest words of condemnation for the religious pride of hypocrites such as the Pharisees. As he made clear in the parable of publican and the Pharisee, those who humble themselves will be exalted, while those who exalt themselves will be humbled (Luke 18:9–14). We are probably more comfortable with examples of humility that are less flamboyant than that of Symeon; nonetheless, Christ's own demonstration of humility was often shocking. Not only did he wash the feet of his disciples, he ate with tax collectors and other known sinners, praised the faith of a centurion, and discussed theology in public with a Samaritan woman. He was accused of demonic possession and heresy, and ultimately died by public execution as a traitor to the Roman Empire.

The Incarnation itself was an act of deep humility, as the Son of God emptied himself of divine glory in order to become a slave, being subject to mortality and to rejection and abuse at the hands of Jewish religious leaders and Gentile political authorities. Contemporary Christians have heard the story of Jesus Christ so often that they may well have lost the ability to be shocked by it and to recognize the astounding humility that is at the heart

---

41. Hesychios the Priest, "On Watchfulness and Holiness," as quoted in Palmer, *The Philokalia* 1, 173.

42. Diadochos of Photiki, "On Spiritual Knowledge and Discrimination," as quoted in Palmer, *The Philokalia* 1, 256.

of their faith. St. Paul made an explicit connection between the meekness of the Lord and the spiritual character required of Christians:

> Let this mind be in you which was also in Christ Jesus, who being in the form of God did not consider it robbery to be equal with God, but made Himself of no reputation, taking the form of a bondservant, and coming in the likeness of men. And being found in appearance as a man, He humbled Himself and became obedience to the point of death, even the death of the cross. (Phil 2:6–8)

The kind of desert monasticism that formed Symeon's spiritual character stressed participation in the humility of Christ, for "God has undergone the vulnerability of assuming child-likeness and death on a cross."[43] Symeon identified with the Lord's self-abnegation by bringing upon himself the rejection and condemnation of the society in which he lived. Christ took upon himself the consequences of all human sin in his death on the cross. The Father "made Him who knew no sin to be sin for us, that we might become the righteousness of God in Him" (2 Cor 5:21). There is something Christ-like in Symeon's giving the impression that he was truly the chief of sinners, someone so corrupt that he was worthy of no one's praise or recognition. Again like Jesus Christ, Symeon's humility enabled him to build relationships with prostitutes and other disreputable people whom he helped to repent and begin living in ways pleasing to God.

Jesus Christ taught that one who cared for "the least of these" in society (e.g., the prisoner, stranger, the sick, and the hungry) actually cared for him; conversely, those who refused to care for such needy persons were guilty of disregarding the Lord (Matt 25:31ff.). Symeon made himself one of "the least of these" so that he could serve Christ in the wretched of his society. His ministry demonstrated the selfless service prized by St. Paul: "Let nothing be done through selfish ambition or conceit, but in lowliness of mind let each esteem others better than himself. Let each of you look out not only for his own interests, but also for the interests of others" (Phil 2:3–4). Symeon's ministry is an icon of radical humility and reminds us that having the humble mind of Christ is a calling for every Christian.

Humility remains an essential characteristic of the Christian life in the contemporary teaching and practice of Eastern Orthodox Christianity. St. Siluoan, a twentieth-century monk who lived on the Orthodox monastic center of Mount Athos, taught that "the soul learns by experience the harm that comes of pride, and so shuns vainglory and the praises of man, and

---

43. Chryssavgis, *In the Heart of the Desert*, 50.

evil thoughts."[44] He insisted that "Only to the humble does the Lord reveal Himself in the Holy Spirit, and if we do not humble ourselves we shall not see God."[45] He distinguished between those who merely know about God and those who truly know God through the personal indwelling of the Holy Spirit. Those without the experiential knowledge of the Holy Spirit enjoy "worldly vanity and praise . . . riches and power; but the Lord is the only desire of the soul that has come to know the Lord through the Holy Spirit, and with her, riches and worldly fame count for naught." Those who know God in this way have learned the humility of Christ and become like him.[46] In contrast, a "proud man fears obloquy, while the humble man cares for nothing . . . it rejoices him to be abused, and grieves him to be acclaimed."[47]

The experiential knowledge of the Holy Spirit that Symeon gained through his decades of prayer and asceticism in the desert enabled him to embody Christ's humility and to have no regard for human praise. His desire to debase himself in the eyes of others was not a form of pathological self-loathing, but instead a spiritual gift that made it possible for him to experience the joy described by Jesus Christ: "Blessed are you when they revile and persecute you, and say all kinds of evil against you falsely for my sake. Rejoice and be exceedingly glad, for great is your reward in heaven . . . " (Matt 5:11–12). From the perspective of Orthodox spirituality, those who do not yet rejoice in such circumstances are in need of further growth in the Christian life, of advancement in holiness. One's relationship with God is dynamic and the journey to "be perfect as your Father in heaven is perfect" is surely an infinite, ongoing endeavor of being purified of sin and sharing by grace in the divine glory that Christ has made available to human beings (Matt 5:48). Siluoan's teaching that humility is the fruit of personal experience of the Holy Spirit serves as a reminder that such lowliness is not a human achievement accomplished by mere self-discipline. Instead, it is truly a gift of God, a dimension of the personal transformation worked by Christ in those who share in his life.

From an Orthodox perspective, those who want to grow in humility should undertake spiritual disciplines that open them to the healing presence of the Holy Spirit. Prayer, fasting, obedience, almsgiving and other forms of service to the needy are methods of learning to resist distorted,

---

44. Sakharov, *Saint Silouan the Athonite*, 298.
45. Ibid., 299.
46. Ibid., 301.
47. Ibid., 308.

self-centered desires and actions that root in pride. Symeon's formation was characterized by severe forms of these disciplines which prepared him for an unusual ministry of mocking the world. The Orthodox Church continues to encourage its members to undertake such basic disciplines, though normally in ways far less demanding than those associated with desert monasticism. Olympic athletes train more strictly than weekend joggers; likewise, hermit monks understandably take their asceticism to greater heights than the average parishioner.

For example, the canons of the Church call for fasting from meat, dairy products, fish, wine, and olive oil on almost all Wednesdays and Fridays of the year, as well as on weekdays throughout the season of Lent and during the shorter fasts in commemoration of the Apostles and the Dormition of the Theotokos in the summer months. Orthodox Christians should fast from meat and dairy throughout the season of Advent, and the last several days before Christmas are observed with the strictness of Lent. Wine and oil, and sometimes fish, are allowed on weekends during these periods, and the guidelines are more lenient for major feast days. Nonetheless, Orthodoxy calls upon everyone in the Church who is physically able to fast from the richest and most satisfying foods with some frequency. With the guidance of their spiritual father or mother, those who are not able to fast from food may instead practice other forms of self-denial.

Additional common spiritual disciplines for Orthodoxy clergy and laity include keeping a daily rule of prayer, taking Confession regularly, forgiving one's enemies, and acts of generosity to the poor. Parish priests encourage the faithful to embrace these disciplines as best they can and in ways appropriate to their present level of spiritual maturity and the challenges posed by the circumstances of their lives. Orthodoxy's ongoing affirmation of asceticism is notable in the self-indulgent culture of the contemporary West. As Metropolitan Kallistos Ware observes, "When all relaxations and dispensations are taken into account, it remains true that Orthodox Christians in the twentieth century—laity as well as monks—fast with a severity for which there is no parallel in western Christendom, except perhaps the strictest Religious Orders."[48]

Few in the Orthodox Church set out intentionally to mock the world, but many dimensions of a seriously Christian life continue to appear foolish in the eyes of dominant cultures, such as love for enemies, generosity

---

48. Ware, *The Orthodox Church*, 300, and *The Orthodox Way*, 116.

to the poor, chastity, and other forms of self-denial done for religious reasons.[49] The middle-class American who pursues a life of missionary service in the developing world, who embraces poverty in order to share the life of homeless people to whom he or she ministers, or who abandons a successful career in order to prepare for virtually any form of church service, does something nonsensical in a culture that prizes monetary gain, social status, and the acquisition of power. From the perspective of those who worship these false gods, I suppose that I am a fool because I have invested my life in the relatively low-paying fields of college teaching and pastoral ministry. (And becoming Eastern Orthodox in Abilene certainly did not increase my social standing!) Christians who struggle for sexual purity, who remain faithful to sick and dying or simply unpleasant spouses, who tithe, or who fast in a serious way, will appear to be idiots from the perspective of those who can imagine nothing more important in life than getting as much pleasure as possible. It would not be hard to cite several other examples of traditional Christian behavior that are radically at odds with the mores of the larger society.

Symeon's radical witness reminds Christians of every variety that the way of the Lord is humble and meek. Those who follow that way will often receive scorn and contempt from others, but strength for such a life of discipleship is found in prayer, fasting, almsgiving, and other spiritual disciplines that facilitate the healing of the soul from the spiritual disease of pride. Symeon's example reflects the truth articulated by Diadochos of Photiki, "Humility is hard to acquire, and the deeper it is, the greater the struggle needed to gain it."[50] Christians seeking an example of how to acquire such humility will do well to look to St. Symeon the Fool for Christ. But if you feel called to throw nuts or otherwise disrupt a church service, please do not show up at St. Luke!

---

49. For accounts of various dimensions of Orthodox praxis that are in tension with dominant cultural norms, see LeMasters, *Toward a Eucharistic Vision of Church, Family, Marriage, and Sex* and *The Goodness of God's Creation*.

50. Diadochos of Photiki, "On Spiritual Knowledge and Discernment," as quoted in Palmer, *The Philokalia* 1, 292.

6

CONSTANTINE AND THE CULTURE WARS

THE PLACE OF CHRISTIANITY in American culture is complicated and probably varies a lot according to region. Where I live in West Texas, most people seem to have no doubt that good Christians vote for the most conservative Republican candidate on the ballot, believe global warming is a hoax, oppose government regulation of the economy, support the death penalty, and own at least one firearm. In Abilene, you will hear explicitly Christian—and often quite lengthy—prayers at public events and real Christmas carols at public school concerts. If there are vocal secularists here, I have never met them. Letters to the editor in the local paper are quite colorful and often proclaim that Democrats and liberals are simply of the devil. In the hardscrabble West of this very red state, we have few religious liberals who champion social spending for the poor, same-sex marriage, legalized abortion, protecting the environment, and opposition to war. The radical left is as rare in my part of the world as statewide office holders who are Democrats. Basically, there aren't any.

Very different are places like California, New York, and Massachusetts, where friends report instances of hostility toward Christianity, especially in its historic forms, and that even Christmas trees are suspect and usually as scarce as Republicans, even moderate ones. They claim that public education teaches their children that the faith is irrational and oppressive. I know a native Texan who works at a firm in the Northeast that always has its staff retreats on Sundays, as the Jewish partners would not participate on Saturdays and hardly anyone involved is a practicing Christian for whom church attendance is a priority. Though I cannot vouch personally for the accuracy of these accounts, which surely paint with a broad brush, they indicate that at least some American believers perceive much more tension than harmony between the local culture and the Christian faith in their neck of the woods.

The relationship between Christianity and culture varies in the United States according to where you are. So we have to be careful in talking about the role of Christianity in "the culture wars" that have received so much attention in the last twenty years. Not everyone is on the same page and facing the same dynamics. Matters become even more complicated when we remember that Eastern Christianity is a new kid on the block when it comes to Western democracy. Centuries of the Byzantine, Russian, and Ottoman empires, as well as decades of deadly oppression by Eastern European Communists, have placed their stamp on the political and cultural sensibilities of Orthodox Christians far more decisively than have the traditions of the United States. Greeks, Russians, Arabs, and others from traditionally Orthodox lands did not come to this country in large numbers until the early decades of the twentieth century. They were typically focused more on preserving their religious and cultural traditions—and putting food on the table—than on political activism. They certainly did not come from parts of the world with thriving Western democracies or anything like American-style separation of church and state.

Some people have the false impression that Eastern Christianity is so otherworldly that it has no interest in the collective life of nations and peoples, while others charge us with "Caesaropapism," which is an awkward way of saying that the Church allows the head of state to order it around. There certainly are examples of political leaders with great influence in the Church for good or bad, but Orthodoxy has powerful spiritual resources to challenge corruption by worldly powers. Granted, those resources are not always used, but they do exist and great saints have suffered and died due to prophetic opposition to political and religious abuses. That is what happened to both St. John Chrysostom, for whom the Divine Liturgy celebrated on most Sundays of the year is named, and for the influential theologian St. Maximus the Confessor, who was horribly mutilated for opposing a heresy supported by an emperor in the seventh century. In the twentieth century, Orthodox believers such as Father Dmitri Klepinin and Mother Maria Skobtsova were martyred in Nazi concentration camps for protecting Jews, while millions of Orthodox clergy, monks, nuns, and laypeople were murdered by Communists for their faith in Eastern Europe.[1] Though he was not martyred, Greek Orthodox Archbishop Iakovos certainly took risks by marching with Dr. Martin Luther King, Jr., at Selma; he was pictured with King on the cover of *Life* magazine.[2]

As with most things Orthodox, we have to go far back in history to get a handle on how the Church interacts with culture. At least since the time of Constantine the Great, the first Christian emperor of Rome in the fourth century, the Orthodox Church has accepted a role in influencing society in ways that are pleasing to God. There is no question that political authorities impact the daily lives of those who live under their rule in many ways. They may do so in a fashion that helps to meet legitimate human needs and to promote the development of a culture that does better rather than worse in serving God's purposes for the collective life of humanity, including treating people with the dignity appropriate to their identity as his children. Out of love for their neighbors, Christians should be supportive of such political and social orders, even as they prod them to do the best they can to promote good and hinder evil.

Even when the Roman Empire was officially pagan, St. Peter urged believers to "Honor the emperor" (1 Pet 2:17). St. Paul wrote to St. Timothy: "I urge that supplications, prayers, intercessions, and thanksgivings be made for all men, for kings and all who are in high places that we may lead a quiet, peaceable life, godly and respectful in every way. This is good, and it is acceptable in the sight of God our Savior, who desires all men to be saved and to come to the knowledge of the truth" (2 Tim 2:1–4). The Lord himself taught to "Render to Caesar the things that are Caesar's, and to God's the things that are God's" (Mark 12:17). Constantine had been a pagan general, but attributed his victories in becoming emperor to the God worshiped by the Christians. Though not baptized until his deathbed, he stopped the persecution of Christians, encouraged and strengthened the Church in many ways, and undertook a number of humanitarian reforms that benefited the weak and vulnerable. The pagan Romans had left their unwanted children to die of exposure or be eaten by animals, enjoyed the bloodshed of gladiatorial games as entertainment, and slaughtered unfortunate groups of men, women, and children when it served their interests. They worshiped notoriously immoral gods and often followed their debauched example.

---

1. Hackel, *Pearl of Great Price*.

2. See Harakas, *Let Mercy Abound*, 33ff., for an account of social concern in the encyclicals of Archbishop Iakovos.

Humility, forgiveness, selfless love, chastity, and generosity to the poor and weak were not their virtues.

In contrast, Constantine and the Christian emperors who followed him made divorce and inheritance laws much fairer for women, protected widows, freed daughters from fathers who prostituted them, and even liberated slave girls from such abuse by their masters.[3] Imperial bans prohibited crucifixion and gladiatorial games. David Bentley Hart notes that Constantine protected married slaves from being separated by their masters and enabled them "to grant slaves their liberty simply by going to church and making the declaration of emancipation before a bishop."[4] Though some of the pagan emperors extended generosity to the poor occasionally, there was "nothing in pagan society remotely comparable to the Christian willingness to provide continuously for persons in need, male and female, young and old, free and bound alike."[5] In a culture where the poor and weak were not treated with any measure of dignity or even humanity, Christianity elevated them to the status of the Body of Christ. Our Savior himself took the form of a slave (Phil 2:6–7). The early Christians knew that what they did to the lowly and vulnerable of their society, they did also to the Lord Jesus (Matt 25). "The flowering of Christian social concern and philanthropy came into being with the legalization and subsequent establishment of the Church in the Christianized Roman Empire . . . . [which produced] hospitals, hospices, homes for the aged, orphanages, houses for the poor, reformatory houses, cemeteries for strangers, and homes[s] for the blind."[6]

Nonetheless, the conversion of the Roman Empire was far from perfect or complete. Constantine did not shed all the pagan trappings of his office or of the empire, probably because doing so was not a political possibility at the time; but he did at times shed blood ruthlessly, even in his own family. He was baptized only on his deathbed, likely in recognition of the grave tension between the morally and spiritually compromised realities of leading the Roman Empire and the demands of following Jesus Christ. Wars, rumors of wars, and human failings of all kinds continued until the final collapse of Constantinople in AD 1453. The Lord said that his Kingdom is not of this world (John 18:36); despite the official Christianity

---

3. David Bentley Hart, *Atheist Delusions*, 160–61. For a popular history of Byzantium, see Lars Brownworth, *Lost to the West*.

4. Hart, *Atheist Delusions*, 162.

5. Ibid., 163.

6. Harakas, *Let Mercy Abound*, 12.

of the Roman Empire, not all was sweetness, light, and holiness. Much of the darkness of the fallen world remained evident. The Church too often failed to fulfill its mission "to sanctify and transform the imperial world order" and too readily accommodated itself to the political expectations of the Empire.[7]

Profound challenges to Christian faithfulness arose with the relative harmony between the Church and the larger culture following Constantine's conversion. No longer was Christian ethics of concern only to Christians as a highly committed religious minority that withstood severe persecution. The temptation was strong to relax the tension between whatever it took to run an earthly kingdom and the teachings of the Sermon on the Mount. Some commentators call this mindset "Constantinianism," a dangerous distortion of the faith and the origin of the error to think that America, capitalism, and Western culture (or whatever political order or ideology we happen to like) are the functional equivalents of God's reign.[8]

There is truth in that criticism, but it is also important not to long romantically for the early centuries of persecution as a golden age of perfection. Christians have lived in fallen cultures from the very beginning. Jesus Christ praised the faith of a Roman centurion, who was an officer in a pagan army of occupation in Palestine (Matt 8:10). There is evidence that some Christians served in the Roman army before Constantine, as many became martyrs when they refused to worship false gods.[9] Abuses of slavery, money, power, and ethnic divisions are clearly evidenced in the New Testament; they have been challenges to the Church from the beginning. What is astonishing, however, is not that Constantine's Roman Empire fell short of manifesting heavenly perfection, but that Christianity was able to impact its culture in such positive ways. The humanitarian reforms of the Christian Roman Empire were without precedent in their day and laid a foundation for respecting human dignity in ways that are still sorely lacking in parts of the world where Christianity is not influential. As Father John McGuckin notes about the Empire's legal heritage,

---

7. Guroian, *Incarnate Love*, 145.

8. See LeMasters, *The Import of Eschatology in John Howard Yoder's Critique of "Constantinianism."*

9. See Helgeland, et al., *Christians and the Military*, for an account of Christian involvement in the military during the first centuries of the Church, as well as Webster, *The Pacifist Option*, 184ff.

> Even when an individual Christian legislation is less than we might have expected it to be (and it certainly took a long time to liberate the slaves, and to raise the educational standards of women in antiquity), the axiomatic compass point is set at the outset. Men and women, of whatever race, or rank, both rich and poor, educated and illiterate, were given equality under the eye of God by this charter. Their lives were raised to infinite value as icons of the divinity, their rights and privileges as the divine icons could never be lost... It is on this basis that Christian civilization was founded ... and which one day may be used once more to rebuild a society's value system.[10]

Of course, the roads, language, and relative stability of Rome also helped the faith to flourish and spread. Just think for a moment how astounding it was for Christianity to move in a matter of a few years from a persecuted minority to the favored religion of the Roman Empire and within a century to its official religion. Despite the imperfections, the Church was blessed through Constantine to enter into a more peaceful period of its history that allowed the faith to prosper. He summoned the Council of Nicaea in AD 325 that produced the basis of the Nicene Creed with its affirmation of the Holy Trinity. That the persecutions ended and the Empire became supportive of Christianity seemed nothing less than miraculous to those who until recently had suffered for their faith.[11] It comes as no surprise, then, that Constantine and his mother Helen are canonized saints of the Orthodox Church.

No doubt, the faith's change in status led to some becoming Christians in name only out of a desire for power and popularity. Nonetheless, many dimensions of the life of the Church continued to highlight the tension between even the Christianized Roman Empire and God's Kingdom. For example, the rise of monasticism around this time stood as a sign of contradiction against the growth of easy, worldly Christianity. Instead of simply equating an officially Christian empire with God's Kingdom, the Church embraced the radical witness of monks and nuns in rejecting of the ways of the world. In the absence of martyrs who literally died at the hands of pagan persecutors, the monastics became living martyrs who died to self as they gave up everything they could in order to follow Christ.

Likewise, the practical necessity of maintaining an army and fighting wars did not lead the Church to ignore the Lord's teaching and example of

---

10. McGuckin, *The Ascent of Christian Law*, 275.
11. See Leithart, *Defending Constantine*.

nonresistant love toward enemies (Matt 5:39). Instead, St. Basil the Great's advice that soldiers who kill in war abstain from taking communion for three years remains part of the canon law of the Orthodox Church, though it is not applied strictly in normal pastoral practice. Monastics and clergy are forbidden to shed blood because killing is incompatible with the ministry of Jesus Christ and a primordial sign of humanity's corruption in a world of sin and death. Their lives are to be straightforward examples of faithful discipleship and taking life—under any circumstances—falls short of the way of the Prince of Peace. The Church tolerates war as a tragic necessity for the protection of the innocent and the vindication of justice, but does not view it as a holy or unambiguously good activity. In sharp contrast with Western Christianity during the Middle Ages, the Eastern Church did not endorse crusades.[12]

The Divine Liturgy includes many petitions for peace, which is more than simply the absence of war or even the presence of a reasonably harmonious social order. Patriarch Bartholomew I of Constantinople writes that "The biblical notion of peace implies the restoration of all things to the original wholeness they enjoyed before the Fall, when man still lived and inhaled the life-giving breath of creation in the image and likeness of God . . . peace is understood as the restoration of the relationship and peace between God and mankind."[13] The Church prays in the Divine Liturgy "for the peace from above and the salvation of our souls," "the peace of the whole world," and "the union of all men."

Christ's peace is not of this world and will be fulfilled only in the coming Kingdom. It is ultimately a characteristic of the fullness of salvation. Nonetheless, even broken and imperfect steps toward reconciliation between enemies are manifestations, no matter how dim, of the Lord's peace. They are steps, no matter how faltering, of the fulfillment of God's purposes for humanity. The Church's witness for peace is not merely to point out the tragic nature of warfare, but to embody practices of reconciliation, forgiveness, and mercy to the suffering that address the underlying causes of hatred, division, and violence. Peacemaking, like the journey of *theosis*, is a dynamic process. Eastern Christianity calls us collectively to become better icons of the blessed fellowship of the Kingdom even as we live in a world that is very far from such heavenly peace.[14]

---

12. LeMasters, "Orthodox Perspectives on Peace, War and Violence," 54–61.
13. Patriarch Bartholomew I, *In the World, Yet Not of the World*, 144.
14. LeMasters, "A Dynamic Praxis of Peace: Orthodox Social Ethics and Just

The wealthy flocked to the Church after Constantine, but the great preachers and saints of the Orthodox Church warned prophetically against the dangers of loving money and ignoring the needy. They also showed the mercy of Christ to the poor in word and deed, even as they reminded the wealthy how hard it is for the rich to enter the Kingdom (Matt 19: 23). For example, St. Basil the Great, St. Gregory the Theologian, and St. Gregory of Nyssa—known as "the Cappadocians"—gave away much of their personal wealth to support "a large complex of buildings that provided shelter for travelers, medical care for the ill—especially . . . lepers, whom society at large despised—food for the hungry, and occupation for many who otherwise would be unemployed."[15] In the Christianized Roman Empire of the fourth century, St. Basil founded the first hospital and the first orphanage in human history, where "the poor and diseased were able to receive food, shelter, and medical treatment free of charge."[16] Byzantine historian Timothy Miller comments that viewing orphans as anything other than property of extended family members was "a Christian idea. The conversion of the Roman Empire to Christianity made a total difference about what to do with people who were unacceptable . . . In classical Greece, an orphan was considered to be disliked by the gods[who] . . . have punished his family or the orphan himself. "[17]

How different was the Christian vision that saw the Lord himself in the poor, needy, and vulnerable. St. Gregory of Nyssa called upon believers to "loosen every bond of injustice, undo the knots of covenants made by force. Break your bread to the hungry; bring the poor and homeless into your house. When you see the naked, cover him; and despise not your own flesh."[18] St. Basil the Great sharply criticized those who selfishly disregard the common purposes for which God created the world's resources: "They seize common goods before others have the opportunity, then claim them as their own by right of preemption. For if we all took only what was necessary to satisfy our own needs, giving the rest to those who lack, no one

---

Peacemaking," 69–82.

15. LeMasters, *The Goodness of God's Creation*, 196.

16. Schroeder, *On Social Justice*, 33.

17. Miller, "Orphanages and Philanthropy in Byzantium," 55.

18. St. Gregory of Nyssa, "The Love of the Poor," as cited in LeMasters, *The Goodness of God's Creation*, 105.

would be rich, no one would be poor, and no one would be in need."[19] To hoard resources when others are in need is simply a violation of justice:

> Is not the person who strips another of clothing called a thief? And those who would not clothe the naked when they have the power to do so, should they not be called the same? The bread you are holding back is for the hungry, the clothes you keep put away are for the naked, the shoes that are rotting away with disuse are for those who have none, the silver you keep buried in the earth is for the needy. You are thus guilty of injustice toward as many as you might have aided, and did not.[20]

St. John Chrysostom was not afraid to call wealthy parishioners to be content with "daily food. I say food, not feasting; raiment, not ornament." He mocked the extravagance of the rich in the face of human suffering: "And your dog is well attended too, while man, or rather Christ . . . is straitened in extreme hunger . . . He that was made in the image of God stands in unseemly plight, through your inhumanity, but the faces of the mules that draw your wife glisten with gold in abundance."[21] The Church's prophetic ministry continued through such bold preaching even after the emperor and the ruling classes had been baptized. These saints went beyond calling for private philanthropy and "also wanted the government to pitch in as well. Saint Basil had no problem in accepting large tracts of imperial land which the emperor Valens gave him to help finance his chartable facilities outside Caesarea."[22]

The circumstances have changed, but the calling remains the same. No matter the society in which they find themselves, the Orthodox faith calls its members to love their neighbors, which certainly entails at least working to meet their basic needs. Because no one is a totally isolated individual, that offering includes our political, cultural, and economic activity, and all our relationships. God calls us to live holy lives and to play our role in the fulfillment of his purposes for the world and all its inhabitants. Salvation is not an escape from the world or other people, but the fulfillment of God's intentions for humans in relation to him, one another, and the

---

19. St. Basil the Great, "I will Tear Down My Barns," 7, in Schroeder, *On Social Justice*, 69.

20. Ibid., 69–70.

21. St. John Chrysostom, "Homily on 2 Corinthians 19:3" and "Homily on Romans 11:5," as cited in LeMasters, *The Goodness of God's Creation*, 108–9.

22. Miller, "Orphanages and Philanthropy in Byzantium," 78.

entire creation. We are created in God's image and likeness, which surely entails treating one another with the dignity of living icons of Christ, as well as doing our best to influence our culture in ways that encourage human flourishing in all respects. If we love our neighbors as ourselves, we will participate in society in ways that help other people lead blessed and holy lives.

The Holy Trinity is the model for all social interaction as a union of distinct persons in love. The Triune God is not a paradigm of domination, but of mutually enriching relationships of those who share a common life while remaining particular persons with freedom and dignity. That is obviously a high goal that is not met perfectly even by faithful members of the Church, but it remains the ultimate norm for all human social interaction in politics, economics, the family, and other spheres. It may seem so high as to be irrelevant, but societies will do a better or worse job of fulfilling God's purposes for humanity and the rest of the creation. No matter where we find ourselves, Christians have a role to play in calling the cultures in which we live to come more fully in line with God's purposes. These are inevitably matters of more or less, not of total good versus complete evil. Even leaving the moral and spiritual ambiguity of warfare aside, it is sobering to remember that the defeat of Nazi Germany and the end of the Holocaust were accomplished by the partnership of Western democracies with Joseph Stalin, the horribly brutal and atheistic dictator of the Soviet Union who severely persecuted Christians. The closer we get to the practical realities of politics and society in our fallen world, the less we find perfection even in the best efforts to establish a tolerable level of justice.

The Byzantines' approach to church-state relations was one of *symphonia* or harmony. Church and state were to co-exist with "mutual respect and dignity" in their respective areas of responsibility toward the flourishing of the society which they both served before God. In the Eastern Roman Empire, citizens were also members of the Church, as was the emperor. Though perfect harmony never existed due to sin and the imperfection of human beings, this approach reflected the view that God's salvation concerns all dimensions of life.[23] Even in the very different circumstances of American culture, Father Alexander Webster warns that it is dangerous to abandon this vision completely because it would divorce basic Christian beliefs from the social and political lives of human beings. He calls for "a political ethics that . . . affirms . . . an organic relationship between the Church and the state,

---

23. Harakas, *Living the Faith*, 348–49.

respects the integrity and freedom of the Orthodox Christian community, and safeguards the religious liberties of non-Orthodox citizens."[24] Surely, to work toward the greatest possible harmony between God's purposes for society and the present realities of culture is one of the callings of the Christian community. As Father Stanley Harakas puts it,

> [W]ithin the *symphonia* [harmony] tradition, the Orthodox layperson living in a democratic society exercises a *political function* analogous to that of the Emperor in the Byzantine experience! Orthodox Christians should learn to translate the ancient imperatives regarding spiritual and moral responsibility for the body politic that were directed to the Emperor to their own political lives. By doing this they will seek to realize them as much as possible in the political system under which they live.[25]

Orthodoxy seeks the salvation of the entire world, the fulfillment of all human beings and the rest of creation in God. Following in the way of Christ's love for humanity, the Church does not accept a radical separation between faith and politics. The Christian witness becomes incarnate in the shared lives of human beings and consequently impacts how they treat one another in social and political matters where the needs of those created in God's image and likeness are at stake. Those who insist that religion has no place in the public square should ponder how impoverished American society would be without the contributions of Christian abolitionists and civil rights activists. Dr. King was, after all, a Baptist preacher.

Defenders of religious liberty need not worry, however, as Eastern Christianity respects the freedom of people to believe as they see fit and certainly does not attempt to impose its doctrines or worship upon anyone by force of law. As Patriarch Bartholomew I of Constantinople states, "Freedom of conscience and the free practice of religious conviction are fundamental principles, which from an Orthodox perspective derive from the words of Jesus Christ: 'Whosoever wants to follow me . . . '"(Matt 16:24).[26]

Precisely how Christians involve themselves in culture will depend upon the particular circumstances that they face and the challenges and opportunities present in given settings. Harsh persecution—which the Eastern Church knows all too well—intensifies the urgency of the fundamental calling of the Church: to keep the faith and model a peaceable and holy way

---

24. Webster, *The Price of Prophecy*, 28–29

25. Harakas, *Living the Faith*, 359.

26. Patriarch Bartholomew I, *Encountering the Mystery*, 137.

of life in stark contrast to the corrupt powers that be. Simply to sustain a community which embodies the spiritual disciplines of Christianity in the face of hostile forces is a major undertaking. Such was the case after the victory of the Ottoman Turks over the Byzantines in AD 1453. For centuries, "The whole Church was placed in a survival stance. The Mohammedan overlords established an Islamic theocracy in which Christians could exist merely as a tolerated minority under severe limitations, exploitation and restrictions."[27] Even under such circumstances, the Greek Orthodox did what they could to care for the poor and sick members of their community, providing dowries to impoverished young women so that they could marry and even establishing hospitals.[28]

Of course, the fundamental practices of the faith—such as prayer, fasting, forgiveness, and caring for the needy—are of equal importance for forming faithful believers in any time and place. In Western democracies where citizens are free to vote, speak, and act according to their consciences, Christians—collectively and individually—may also act within broad constraints to bear witness in and transform the larger society by means of activism. For example, attorneys associated with Orthodox Christians for Life submitted a friend of the court brief to the United States Supreme Court on behalf of the Church in an effort to overturn *Roe V. Wade* as "a gruesome turn on the road of judicial activism, having resulted in a holocaust which has claimed at least twenty million innocent lives."[29] Several Orthodox clergy and laity signed "The Manhattan Declaration," a conservative Christian statement against abortion and euthanasia and in defense of traditional marriage and religious liberty.[30] The Assembly of Canonical Orthodox Bishops of North and Central America likewise appealed to religious liberty in calling on the Obama administration to rescind its ruling that Roman Catholic-related institutions must pay for contraception and sterilization for their employees, regardless of that church's moral opposition to these practices.[31] The National Religious Campaign Against Torture

---

27. Harakas, *Let Mercy Abound*, 14.

28. Ibid., 17.

29. See "An Orthodox View of Abortion: The *Amicus Curiae* Submitted to the Supreme Court." This brief was submitted by Orthodox Christians for Life with the endorsement of various Orthodox jurisdictions represented in the US.

30. See "The Manhattan Declaration."

31. "Record of Protest Against the Infringement of Religious Liberty by the Department of Health and Human Services."

has received endorsement and support from Orthodox leaders.[32] The Orthodox Peace Fellowship of North America issued an appeal to President George W. Bush expressing opposition to the invasion of Iraq in 2003.[33] Working to bring the practices of society and government into greater harmony with God's purposes for humanity is a virtuous endeavor that is in keeping with the spiritual and social vision of Orthodoxy, despite the inevitable limitations and imperfections of fallen humanity's collective life.

Christians must do what they can to be salt and light in a dark, decaying world where the consequences of sin and corruption are often all too evident (Matt 5:13–16). For example, the Orthodox Church is the largest Christian body in Syria, which has a total Christian population of less than 10 percent. As of this writing, the civil war between President Assad's government and the rebels continues to rage. Syria has no real democratic traditions and the government is by all accounts a brutal dictatorship. There are very few models of governments and societies in the Middle East that treat human beings decently and the persecution of Christians of all varieties is pervasive. In this setting of very limited options, Syria's Christians have been generally supportive of Assad because he has protected them from religious persecution at the hands of the majority Sunni Muslim population. So the Church in Syria does what it can to provide humanitarian relief to refugees, as well as to other victims of the fighting, and to call for peace. It does not pretend to be a powerbroker or an influential force in partisan politics, but acts to encourage dialogue and reconciliation between enemies. What the future holds for these believers is uncertain and we should all remember them in our prayers. As in other violent situations, simply to sustain the basic practices of the Church as a communal witness to God's reign becomes a major undertaking. St. Paul's admonitions in Romans 12–13 affirm both submission to the governing authorities and self-sacrificial love and forgiveness toward all, including enemies and persecutors. The difficult road walked by the Orthodox of Syria is as old as Christianity itself.

Eastern Christians are obviously a small minority in the United States and do not play a visible or powerful role in shaping the larger culture. A few Orthodox politicians have risen to national prominence, such as Democrat

32. "National Religious Campaign Against Torture."

33. See "A Plea for Peace from the Orthodox Peace Fellowship of North America." Webster, *The Price of Prophecy*, 333, concludes that "The Orthodox jurisdictions in the United States have yet to demonstrate moral maturity" in responding to social and political challenges.

presidential nominee Governor Michael Dukakis and Republican Senator Olympia Snowe, but the Church does not present itself as a partisan force in American politics. Orthodox bishops gave invocations at the national conventions of both major political parties in 2012. Personally, I know more Orthodox who are Republicans than Democrats, which is not surprising at least in part because I live in Texas. Though there are many reasons why people affiliate with political parties, the Church's official stances on abortion, euthanasia, homosexuality, and same-sex marriage certainly have more in common with the current platform of the GOP on these hot button issues than with that of the Democrats. Nonetheless, the Church does not give official directives on how its members should vote in particular elections, and there is no one-to-one correspondence between the social vision of the Church and that of any political interest group. As Rod Dreher states about academicians who have converted to Orthodoxy in the US, "Though many vote Republican, nearly all the conservative intellectuals I spoke with . . . express gratitude that Orthodoxy avoids the 'Republican Party at prayer' feeling that pervades some Evangelical churches."[34]

Orthodox clergy and laity are rarely prominent players or partisans in the culture wars on controversial issues. Of course, given the obscurity of Eastern Christianity in American society, it would be odd for Orthodoxy to be highly visible in the larger culture in any way. The movie *My Big Fat Greek Wedding* probably remains the high-water mark of Orthodoxy's presence in the public eye. Tom Hanks, Tina Fey, and Jennifer Aniston are certainly well-known entertainers, but they are rarely identified as members of the Orthodox Church. And only people of a certain age remember the late actors Telly Savalas, Yul Brynner, Natalie Wood, and John Belushi, all of whom were Eastern Christians.

There are certainly different ways for a church to attempt to bear witness in its local culture; those methods have their respective strengths and weaknesses. For example, to become so insular that the Church's ministry extends no further than the walls of the building in the name of sectarian purity amounts to a failure to recognize God's concern for all dimensions of life and for every human being. Christ's Kingdom is not of this world, but it is also not irrelevant for people who live and breathe in the world as we know it, regardless of their religion. "Let your light so shine before men that they may see your good works and give glory to your Father who is in heaven" (Matt 5:16). We will not fulfill the Lord's command by withdrawing

---

34. Dreher, "Eastern Right: Conservative Minds Convert to Orthodox Christianity."

from engagement with the real-life challenges that impact our neighbors so directly. Hiding our light under a bushel is not an option. As Vigen Guroian writes, Orthodox "sectarian retreat" would amount to "a refusal to articulate a real social ethic, even by the measure of its own incarnational faith, which has always taken the world itself to be the matter of the sacrament of the Kingdom."[35]

Conversely, to align the faith closely with particular political parties or partisan movements is to risk substituting the calling to *theosis* with that of being a certain kind of citizen, voter, or activist. In the current cultural climate of the US, there are potential dangers to a close affiliation of Eastern Christianity with the stereotypically liberal, moderate, conservative, or libertarian movements of American politics. The faith does not fit perfectly with any such orientation; likewise, the Church is not a political party. The Body of Christ ultimately pursues the Kingdom of God, not merely a different arrangement of the kingdoms of this world. Its social vision is not the product of twenty-first-century America or the collection of interest groups that comprise our political movements, but grows from ancient and diverse sources that do not line up squarely with any worldly ideology. Orthodoxy's social and moral concerns are in tension with much popular political opinion of whatever stripe.

As well, the Church's cultural presence does not boil down to a collection of statements on issues, but is a function of its witness as "a community of faith whose very character sets it apart from the world with its passing powers, principalities, and ideologies." As Guroian comments, "There is no easy or consistent correlation of the values and virtues of the Kingdom with those of even so amorphous an ideology as that of liberal democracy. The greatest service the Church can do for any worldly organization is to address that organization as the very presence of the Kingdom in its midst."[36] The Church seeks to act and speak as a sign of God's eschatological salvation and consequently sees many matters in a different light from conventional political discourse. Calling the world to holiness takes precedence over pursuing a more just arrangement of worldly powers.

For example, there is a notable current of thought against the death penalty in Orthodoxy. St. Vladimir abolished it in the ninth century upon his conversion and several contemporary Orthodox bishops and jurisdictions have called for the abolition of capital punishment. Jesus Christ, of

---

35. Guroian, *Incarnate Love*, 129.
36. Ibid., 126.

course, stopped the stoning of the woman caught in adultery with the admonition that she "go and sin no more" (John 8:11). St. Nicholas of Myra, the real Santa Claus, stopped three executions in the fourth century. Though there are surely a variety of opinions about capital punishment among Orthodox Christians and no officially binding teaching, opposition to the death penalty in the Church focuses on the Lord's mercy to sinners and the possibility of repentance even by those who have committed the most heinous crimes.[37] One rarely encounters such a spiritually informed stance that challenges the widespread acceptance of the practice in the US.

The Lord's baptism in the Jordan River grounds the ecological concern of Eastern Christianity, as the Son of God blessed and made holy the water—and by implication the entire creation—when he was baptized in it.[38] At every vespers (evening prayer) service, we read Psalm 104, which blesses God for the wonders of the natural world. The holy mysteries or sacraments of the Church use water, wine, bread, and oil to make present the Lord's mercy in tangible, physical ways. These elements are all products of the Earth in one way or another and remind us that it is through God's creation (of which we are a part) that we will find salvation. Adam's first calling was to be a good steward of the earth, and Christians err when they forget that salvation is the fulfillment—not the destruction—of their Father's world. Jesus Christ entered the physical creation at his birth and he ascended with a glorified human body into heaven. St. Paul wrote that "the whole creation has been groaning in travail together until now" (Rom 8:22).

My meager ecological efforts include recycling, composting, and driving a hybrid, all of which make me a flaming radical by West Texas standards. Because of the deep theological grounding of Eastern Christianity's ecological concerns, Patriarch Bartholomew I of Constantinople, known as "the Green Patriarch," is an outspoken advocate of efforts to control carbon emissions as a way of fighting global warming.[39] He also sees environmental stewardship as closely related to whether we really love and serve both God and our neighbors:

> What we do for the earth is intimately related to what we do for people . . . whether with regard to poverty or social justice or

---

37. "Orthodoxy and Capital Punishment."

38. See Theokritoff, *Living in God's Creation* and LeMasters, *The Goodness of God's Creation*, 1ff.

39. See "Orthodoxy and the Environment" and Chryssavgis, *Cosmic Grace, Humble Prayer*.

world peace. It has become clearer to us that the way we respond to the natural environment is intimately and deeply connected to the way we treat human beings . . . Therefore, the willingness of some people to exploit the environment, which is the "flesh of the world," goes hand in hand with their willingness to ignore human suffering in the flesh of our neighbor. And, by the extension, the willingness to respond to the needs of creation and of our neighbor reflects our willingness to respect the way of the heart and the commandments of God.[40]

Orthodox sensibilities go beyond theologically shaped reservations about the death penalty and concern for global warming to address the troubled history of the Middle East. Especially shocking to many evangelicals will be Eastern Christianity's lack of enthusiasm about the State of Israel and Zionism. The most fundamental point here is that Jesus Christ had no interest in establishing an earthly kingdom for Jews or anyone else (e.g., John 18:36). St. Paul stressed that the Lord broke down the division between Jew and Gentile (e.g., Eph 2:14; Gal 3:23-29). The first generations of believers clearly included Gentiles who lived in Palestine (e.g., John 4:7ff; Acts 6:5ff; 10:44ff; 15:1ff.). Though their number has shrunk due to persecution by various groups and governments, the Middle East is still home to millions of Christians who trace their ancestry back to the first centuries of the Church.

Basic New Testament teachings emphasize the fulfillment of God's promises to Abraham in Jesus Christ, who is the Savior of all who come to him in faith and repentance. Old Testament prophecies point to the coming of the Messiah, not to establishment of the kind of religious-ethnic kingdom that the Messiah refused to set up. Consequently, the contemporary nation of Israel has no particular theological significance for Orthodox Christians. St. Peter referred to the Church—not the citizens of an earthly kingdom or those with a given ethnic heritage—as "a chosen race, a royal priesthood, a holy nation, God's own people" (1 Pet 2:9). St. Paul stressed that God's promises to the descendants of Abraham are fulfilled in Jesus Christ, in whom they extend to all who have faith (e.g., Gal 3:6-9). He taught that Gentile Christians "are no longer strangers and sojourners, but . . . fellow citizens with the saints and members of the household of God . . . " (Eph 2:19).

---

40. Patriarch Bartholomew I, *In the World, Yet Not of the World*, 201.

Likewise, he wrote that "not all who are descended from Israel belong to Israel . . . the children of the promise are reckoned as descendents" (Rom 9:6–8). "It is men of faith who are the sons of Abraham," he reminded the Galatians (Gal 3:7). Those who have faith in the Savior "are Abraham's offspring, heirs according to the promise" (Gal 3:29). Consequently, Eastern Christianity calls both Jews and Gentiles to embrace the good news of God's salvation in Jesus Christ. As St. Paul taught, part of the mission of the Church is "to make Israel jealous" so that the Jews will accept the fulfillment of their blessed heritage in the Messiah (Rom 11:11).

Patriarch Bartholomew I states that "We respect the role of Israel as a guarantor of the Jewish people's existence."[41] But like any other nation, Israel should act in accordance with international law in relation to other nations, withdraw from illegally occupied areas, and treat all within its borders with equal human dignity. The Palestinians have as much right to their own state as do the Israelis. The intentional harassment suffered by Arab Christians in Israeli-occupied areas such as Bethlehem is both horrendous and little known in America. Arbitrary checkpoints, walls that make travel to jobs, hospitals, and schools virtually impossible, confiscation of land, and other indignities are accomplishing their intended goal of making life so hard for Arab Christians that many of them emigrate. In some parts of Jerusalem, it is common for Jews to spit upon the cross and Christian clergy when they encounter them in public. The Israeli government makes it very difficult for Palestinian believers even to visit the Christian holy sites to which tourists from other countries have easy access.[42]

Contrary to popular assumptions, criticism of these policies is certainly not the same as supporting terrorism, anti-Semitism, or war against Israel. Like all the Christian bodies in Israel and Palestine, the Orthodox Church wants its members to live in peace and harmony with their neighbors, regardless of their religion. The Kairos Palestine document "A Moment of Truth: A Word of Faith, Hope, and Love from the Heart of Palestinian Suffering" is a statement from the leaders of those churches that combines a call for justice with a clear commitment to nonviolent resistance and forgiving love.[43] The recent statement of the Assembly of Canonical Orthodox Bishops of North and Central America makes a similar appeal concerning

---

41. Ibid., 92.

42. See Maria Khoury, "Taybeh's Plea for the Last Christians of the Holy Land."

43. See "A Moment of Truth: A Word of Faith, Hope, and Love from the Heart of Palestinian Suffering," 1–16.

situations of persecution and injustice in the Middle East and around the world:

> Finally, we pray for our oppressed and suffering brothers and sisters variously facing oppression or persecution in the ancient Patriarchates of Constantinople, Alexandria, Antioch, and Jerusalem, as well as in the Balkans and throughout the world. We grieve the loss of US Ambassador Christopher Stevens and his staff in Libya. We condemn all forms of violence perpetrated in the name of religion and denounce all expressions of religious intolerance. *Now may the Lord of peace Himself grant you peace at all times in all ways. The grace of our Lord Jesus Christ be with you all* (2 Thess 3.16, 18)."[44]

I know many Arab Christians through our Antiochian Orthodox Archdiocese, which is under the spiritual authority of Patriarch John X of Antioch, who is located in Damascus, Syria. Some are Palestinians, including a peace activist whom I met at a conference in Greece. She reports that when she encounters Western Christians, they are usually shocked to meet an Arab who is not a Muslim. They ask her, "When did you become a Christian?" She responds, "My people have been Christians for two thousand years." A similar ignorance exits in Abilene. When I told an acquaintance that our parish has an Arab Christian heritage, he asked if many Muslims attend our services. "No," I replied, "that's a different religion." Muslims, not all Arabs, practice Islam. One would hope most people knew that already.

The cultural sensibilities of Eastern Christians led several Orthodox bishops in America and around the world to question the wisdom of the invasion of Iraq in 2003. As Metropolitan Philip, the archbishop of Antiochian Archdiocese in North America, wrote to President Bush, "We are gravely concerned, however, that a war against Iraq will create even more chaos in the region. The overthrowing of the Iraqi government could cause the breakup of the country into warring factions for many years to come. In addition, the geo-political imbalance this war would cause in the area will take generations to repair.[45] Recent years have shown that the Metropolitan's concerns were justified. In the aftermath of the civil unrest following the invasion, the Christian population of Iraq has fallen by more than half. Prospects for a peaceful democracy that respects the human dignity of all

---

44. Assembly of Canonical Orthodox Bishops of North and Central America, "Message to the Faithful."

45. See Saliba, "On Iraq: Statement Issued by Metropolitan Philip."

citizens seem dim. Likewise, I do not know anyone who is pleased by the growing power of Iran in the region, which is at least in part the result of the instability of Iraq. These judgments are not official teachings of the Church and there are Orthodox who disagree with them; still, they serve as examples of distinctive insights that Eastern Christians may bring to the American public square in light of their history and culture.[46]

How sad that the policy makers of the West rarely pay attention to—or are even aware of—the perspectives of Christians from the Middle East. That is a tendency that goes back many centuries. Some historians maintain that the victims who suffered most from the Western crusades of the Middle Ages were the Eastern Christians. Not only did the Fourth Crusade in AD 1204 sack Constantinople and set the stage for the collapse of the Byzantine Empire to the Ottoman Turks in AD 1453, Orthodox bishops were often replaced by Roman Catholic ones in areas conquered by the crusaders.[47] As hard as it is for us in the West to understand, the memory of the Crusades is alive and well in the Middle East and in the memory of the Eastern Church. Contemporary controversies in that part of the world look different from a perspective shaped by the struggles of Christians who are indigenous to the region. Orthodoxy does not see the world simply through the eyes and experiences of Western culture and thus offers a unique perspective on a very important part of the world.

Orthodox perspectives on money are also not simply the product of Western experience. The sensibilities of the Church are not identical with those who insist on a given economic philosophy, including an unrestricted free market, as being the best for all times and places. Orthodoxy has thrived—or at least endured—in settings with a wide variety of social and economic systems. The Church does not dictate any given ideology about these matters as the perfect way of the Kingdom of God. The bounty of the Earth is God's blessing to all, but wealth should never be an end in itself or become a false god. No matter how a given society handles property, labor, and commerce, God's claim on the creation trumps ours and we should use his world to serve his purposes, not simply our own. Created in the divine image and likeness, human beings are persons who flourish together in community, while respecting the freedom and uniqueness of each person. A social order that eliminates the freedom, responsibility, and initiative

---

46. See Webster and Cole, *The Virtue of War*, for a contrasting perspective on the "war on terror."

47. See Papadakis and Meyendorff, *The Christian East and the Rise of the Papacy*, 69ff.

of particular people in relation to their work and welfare falls short of respecting the personal nature of human beings. Likewise, a culture that prizes selfishness, conspicuous consumption, and lack of concern for needy neighbors and the common good fails to recognize that people are persons in relationship with others, not simply isolated individuals.

The spiritual teachers of Eastern Christianity call for those with adequate resources to meet their basic needs and give what is left over to the poor. We are called to stewardship of the common blessings of God's creation in ways that are good for all, not to self-centered indulgence. As the Assembly of Canonical Orthodox Bishops of North and Central America recently stated, "We must resist the wastefulness and greed that dominate our consumer society, confessing that our spiritual *citizenship is in heaven* (Phil 3:20) in order that our witness be characterized by the compassion and mercy as well as the generosity and philanthropy that distinguishes our God who loves humankind."[48]

There is solid basis, then, for Orthodox criticism of both excessive state control and unbridled capitalism, as well as of stances in between those extremes. In contrast to those who insist that only private organizations should engage in social work, Father Harakas rejects the view that government social service programs are the result of the failure of the churches to exercise proper philanthropy. Instead, the rise of public assistance may be seen

> as a victory of the Church in which the Church's values of philanthropy, love, and caring have been assumed and adopted by society at large and by the state in particular. As such, the Church rejoices in the fact that the state is not indifferent to its poor, its suffering, its weak, its minorities and those incapable of caring for themselves. Consequently, the Church ought not to deplore the assumption by the state of much of the philanthropic work formerly done by the Church.[49]

As mentioned earlier, Orthodoxy takes traditional positions on questions of sexuality and the protection of life that sharply contradict so-called progressive trends. When I spoke at an ecumenical peacemaking conference a few years ago, I asked a representative from a mainline Protestant denomination why no one at the conference ever mentioned abortion as a form of violence to be overcome. He said that such concerns simply

---

48. "Message to the Faithful."
49. Harakas, *Living the Faith*, 363.

are not part of the progressive agenda. Orthodoxy views the matter quite differently.

The Church follows the teaching and example of historic Christianity in rejecting abortion and calling for repentance and spiritual healing even in the tragic case of a pregnant woman who saves her own life by terminating that of her unborn child.[50] From the first century to the present day, Eastern Christianity has viewed abortion as always gravely sinful. *The Didache* and *The Epistle of Barnabas*, both written within the first century of Christianity, state "Do not murder a child by abortion, nor kill it at birth."[51] Modern science verifies that the growth of the fetus is a continuous process of the development of a human being. Eastern Christianity has never recognized a point in fetal development before which the unborn baby is anything but one of us—a person created in the image and likeness of God.[52] Jesus Christ was once an unborn child who sanctified the womb, as he did all of human existence. The Orthodox calendar not only commemorates his conception at the feast of the Annunciation, but also celebrates feasts for the conception of St. John Baptist and Mary the Theotokos. These commemorations underscore the Church's belief that children in the womb are distinct persons before God. St. Luke's account of the unborn St. John the Baptist leaping in the womb to greet the unborn Jesus Christ makes that point quite clearly (Luke 1:41). How we treat unborn children, who are very much "the least of these" in the eyes of the world, is how we treat our Savior, who identified himself with the weak and vulnerable throughout his ministry.

From the origins of the faith, Christians learned to see the Lord in those whom the powerful of the world disregarded. They saw that slaves, abandoned children, and the poor, for example, have the same dignity in Christ as anyone else who bears the divine image and likeness. God's love for humanity extends to all, even to the defenseless human beings growing in the womb. The Church's opposition to abortion is not some extraneous quirk added to the faith in order to control women's bodies. It is, instead, an intrinsic dimension of Christ-like love for those waiting to be born in precisely the way that the Savior did. As Guroian comments,

---

50. See Breck, *The Sacred Gift of Life*, 146ff.

51. *The Didache*, 2, and *The Epistle of Barnabas*, 19.5, as cited in Sparks, *The Apostolic Fathers*, 298, 309.

52. See Engelhardt, *The Foundations of Christian Bioethics*, 275.

> In point of fact, the statements about abortion in the letters of St. Basil or the homilies of St. John Chrysostom were not intended to be metaphysical pronouncements about the beginnings of human life. Nor are they statements about basic human rights in the profoundest sense . . . They are primarily exhortations directed to a specific community about what kind of a people it is and what behavior is or is not fitting with its identity as the bride of Christ and the sacrament of the Kingdom of Trinitarian love open to all life.[53]

Contrary to partisan political rhetoric, this stance does not degrade women, but instead values and affirms their unique dignity as those who bring life into the world through their own bodies. Those who devalue pregnancy by viewing abortion as just another medical procedure that an isolated individual may demand on the basis of rights actually devalue women, children, and the family. If unborn children have so little standing that they may be destroyed at will, without even the knowledge of the father, why should men accept any responsibility for their children or the women who carry them? And why should the needs of pregnant women receive any particular consideration in society? The logic of many of the same arguments used to justify abortion also support infanticide. If a society sees no intrinsic dignity in life in the womb and accepts the deliberate killing of unborn children, what other classes of human beings will be in jeopardy?

American culture has moved in the wrong direction on these matters. Rather than finding ways to make it easier for women to have abortions or celebrating the right to destroy unborn children, a humane society will extend protection for life in the womb even as it finds ways to help women in difficult circumstances welcome their babies. To discourage abortion and encourage men and women to take responsibility for the children that they conceive is a fundamental building block of a society that respects the dignity of human beings. As the Assembly of Canonical Orthodox Bishops of North and Central America recently stated, "We must strive to eliminate the violence proliferated against innocents of every kind, particularly of women and the unborn. We call for responsibility by individuals, institutions and governments to ensure the welfare of every citizen."[54]

Unfortunately, partisan politics has obscured thoughtful, yet alone spiritually-informed, conversations about the dignity of life in the womb

---

53. Guroian, *Incarnate Love*, 126.
54. "Message to the Faithful."

and the difficult circumstances that lead women to seek abortions. Politicians of whatever ideological persuasion use the issue as red meat to stoke the enthusiasm of their respective bases. It is ironic that those who otherwise favor government intervention to protect the weak often defend absolute abortion rights as a matter of individual liberty, while those who oppose government regulation of the economy or gun ownership often call for legal prohibition of abortion. Instead of engaging in interminable debates about who has a right to what, Eastern Christianity asks what actions are in keeping with love for our neighbors, including the child in the womb, the pregnant woman, the father, and others involved in the situation. Christians should treat all concerned with the love and dignity that they would show to the Lord himself. The fundamental challenges here go much deeper than political advocacy to forming the hearts and souls of human beings through the life of the Church, as well as modeling to the larger society what it means to welcome children and to support pregnant women and their families. Apart from such a witness, Christians will not be able to play their legitimate role in raising the level of society's discussion about abortion.

Likewise, the Church clearly opposes "mercy killing" or euthanasia that would end the lives of patients in order to put them out of their misery. Refusing pointless, overly burdensome, or spiritually unhealthy treatment is legitimate and in some cases obligatory. But intentionally seeking to kill a patient is a form of murder, a violation of the most fundamental commitments of health care, and a repudiation of the example of Christ's compassionate healing ministry.[55] Like unborn children, patients who are dying or suffering horribly are inconvenient and expensive; they are among the most vulnerable members of society. Many people in such circumstances are not in full possession of their mental faculties; consequently, they are easily subject to abuse—even by those who stand to inherit their possessions or want to give their hospital beds to someone else. True Christian compassion embraces these patients and provides whatever comfort is possible to the suffering and weak; it does not try to kill them or get them out of the way.

Some argue for euthanasia out of a misguided sense of compassion. Patients who want euthanasia often do so because they are alone, in pain, and see no worth in continuing a pointless existence. The hospice

---

55. See Breck, *The Sacred Gift of Life*, 203ff; Engelhardt, *Foundations of Christian Bioethics*, 327ff.

movement addresses many of these concerns. Hospice provides palliative care to dying patients when more aggressive treatment has become pointless or overly burdensome, often allowing a patient to die at home, in the presence of loved ones, and without the nuisance of intrusive machines and tubes. Many health care providers believe that American physicians are not well-trained in the use of pain medication and are reluctant to prescribe sufficient doses due to fear of patients becoming addicted or having adverse reactions. A more appropriate use of pain medication to make terminal patients comfortable would likely decrease the demand for euthanasia. A welcome ministry in the Orthodox Church would be to develop hospice units and other settings for patients to end their earthly lives in peace as they prepare to enter into the presence of the Lord. At the very least, Orthodox health care professionals should make of their healing work a sign of Christ's steadfast compassion for the sick and dying.[56]

If abortion and euthanasia are not sufficiently controversial, let's turn to the ethics of sex. The Church has always affirmed that marriage is between one man and one woman, viewing sexual intimacy outside of this union as sinful. There is simply no record or tradition of the Church blessing other kinds of marital arrangements. Likewise, the Church has always taught that unmarried persons—regardless of their age or sexual inclinations—should abstain from intimate relations. That is not because sex is somehow evil, but because the uniquely life-giving union of man and woman is unspeakably holy and a sign of the relationship between Christ and the Church (Eph 5:22–23). Orthodox Christians marry in the Church, receiving the blessing of the Lord and wearing ceremonial crowns which show that marriage is an icon of the salvation of the Kingdom of heaven, as well as a form of martyrdom in which we die to self out of love for God and one another.

The Church blesses marriages not simply—or even primarily—to encourage parents to stay together to raise their children. Instead, the intimate and life-giving union of man and woman is an image of the relationship between Christ and the Church. He often used the wedding feast as a symbol of the Kingdom of God; it was at a wedding feast that he turned water into wine (John 2:1–11). Likewise, the troubled relationship of male and female finds healing and fulfillment in Christ. With one another and their children, man and woman are called to grow in holiness and find salvation. Sexual intimacy and all its fruits find their proper place in this

---

56. See LeMasters, *The Goodness of God's Creation*, 60ff.

blessed life-giving union of the two kinds of human beings created together in God's image (Gen 1:27–28).

Widows, divorced persons, single moms and dads, extended family members, and others may find themselves raising children alone. The Orthodox Church includes many people in that situation and wishes them every success. My experience is that parishes do what they can to help kids and those who raise them do the very best that they can in life, regardless of the circumstances. Nonetheless, the ideal environment for rearing our young remains a family with a mother and father united by the lifelong commitment of marriage. Husband, wife, and child image the Holy Trinity as a union of persons in love that brings forth new life. How sad that so many today find such a vision to be unrealistic and outdated. To hold up this high vision is certainly in no way to condemn those in other circumstances or to recognize that many face them through no fault of their own. It is also not to deny that there are married couples who are lousy parents and unmarried people who do a much better job of raising their children. Churches and societies that do not recognize the unique glory of marriage and family will be much the poorer for it, however, as rates of poverty, abuse, and other challenges in single-parent homes sadly make clear.

A key underlying point of Orthodox teaching about these matters is the marital nature of sexual intercourse. For St. Paul, even a casual encounter with a prostitute results in the "one flesh" union (1 Cor 6:16). And try as we might to deny it, the biological realities of sex tend in the usual order of things toward pregnancy. To reserve baby-making activity for the committed union of marriage is the best approach for all concerned. Unlike some more liberal religious bodies, Orthodoxy did not change its moral teachings in response to the sexual revolution. It may not be popular, but the ancient Christian truth remains that God intends man and woman to become one flesh only in the lifelong covenant of marriage. Anything less is a cheap substitute that wreaks havoc with hearts, souls, bodies, children, and families. Both rap and country music provide ample evidence of this claim.

It is very hard to discern out how to address these matters in a culture as confused as ours about sex. Many dismiss traditional Christian teaching as outdated moralism, self-righteous hypocrisy, or part of a reactionary political agenda. The public square lacks a language to discuss sex as anything other than a matter of public health, biological function, or rights. The essayist Wendell Berry hits the nail on the head when it comes to the dangers of reducing matters of sex to conventional political categories of liberal versus conservative:

> The "conservatives" more or less attack homosexuality, abortion, and pornography, and the "liberals" more or less defend them. Neither party will oppose sexual promiscuity. The "liberals" will not oppose promiscuity because they do not wish to appear intolerant of "individual liberty." The "conservatives" will not oppose promiscuity because sexual discipline would reduce the profits of corporations, which in their advertisements and entertainments encourage sexual self-indulgence as a way of selling merchandise.[57]

In sharp contrast, Eastern Christianity views promiscuity, personal freedom, and the commercialization of sex in light of the vocation of man and woman to image the life of the Holy Trinity through their intimate union and spiritual, familial, and social offspring. Something more profound than the usual political and moral rhetoric of American interest groups is necessary to direct our deep desires for intimacy in ways that are good for all concerned and teach us to love God with every ounce of our being. To pretend that nothing more is at stake here than the freedom of consenting adults or the commercial reality that sex sells is to pursue a spiritual and moral dead end that poses serious obstacles to the pursuit of a holy—or even a decent—life for this and future generations.

In contrast to the current trends of American culture, Eastern Christianity has never endorsed same-sex marriage and from its origins has viewed homosexual intimacy as sinful.[58] When answering a question about divorce, Jesus Christ affirmed that "from the beginning God made them male and female. 'For this reason a man shall leave his father and mother and be joined to his wife, and the two shall become one flesh.' So they are no longer two but one flesh" (Mark 10:6–8). He did not specifically address the morality of same-sex relations, probably because there was a consensus in Judaism that such acts were an abomination before God. That is why St. Paul could use both male and female homosexuality as obvious examples of the consequences of the Gentiles' idolatry in Romans 1:26–28. When the Lord addressed matters of marital fidelity in the Sermon on the Mount, he intensified the Old Testament law by teaching that "everyone who looks at a woman lustfully has already committed adultery with her in his heart"

---

57. Berry, *Sex, Economy, Freedom and Community*, 123.
58. See LeMasters, *Toward a Eucharistic Vision of Church, Family, Marriage, and Sex*, 79ff.

(Matt 5:27). Jesus Christ did not relax the ancient laws about sex and marriage; instead, he strengthened them.[59]

By those standards, it is clear that we have all sinned and fallen short of the glory of God (Rom 3:23). As St. Paul wrote after his description of human depravity, "Therefore you have no excuse, O man, whoever you are, when you judge another; for in passing judgment upon him you condemn yourself, because you, the judge, are doing the very same things" (Rom 2:1). Surely, everyone struggles with unholy sexual passions in one way or another and there is no room for self-righteous condemnation in genuine Christianity. The Church provides the same compassion to gays and lesbians that it provides to anyone else who struggles with temptation and humbly asks for God's mercy when they sin. Orthodoxy is not homophobic in the sense of having an irrational fear or hatred of people who find themselves attracted to members of the same sex or somehow disconnected from their own male or female bodies. When parishioners go to their priest for counseling on how to lead a holy life and grow as Christians, they receive guidance on how to fight their passions and gain the spiritual strength necessary to abstain from unholy sexual acts of whatever variety. When people stumble and truly repent, spiritual fathers assure them of God's forgiveness and help them to get back up and move forward step by step. The focus is on the journey to *theosis,* not an unhealthy obsession about sexual desires of any kind.

A friend suggests that pastors not preach against homosexuality, as such sermons tempt at least 90 percent of the congregation to self-righteousness. His point is provocative, as all the attention given to this controversial topic directly impacts the concerns of a very small portion of society. Likewise, it is not as though churches of any variety are such bastions of chastity that most members have energy to spare worrying about other people's most intimate struggles. We need to remove the logs from our own eyes before we try to remove a speck from someone else's (Matt 7:3). If traditional Christian teaching on sexuality presents itself simply as a word of condemnation and judgment for gays and lesbians, who can blame them—and their family members, friends, and supporters—for failing to see that the faith is good news? Regardless of our problems with sex or anything else, all human beings bear the image and likeness of God and should be treated accordingly. Everyone is called to a life of holiness and the joy of eternal life already in this world. We must embody Christ's love, humility,

---

59. See Gagnon, *The Bible and Homosexual Practice,* 227–28; 264ff.

and chastity if we are to be of help to anyone else. If not, we become just like the self-righteous, hypocritical Pharisees who rejected the Savior.

These matters are best dealt with in the confidentiality of confession and pastoral counseling, not by political activism that reduces deep spiritual realities to partisan rhetoric. The recent statement of American Orthodox bishops sets the right tone: "We must safeguard the sacrament of marriage in accordance with God's will for the sacred union between man and woman and the sanctity of family as the fundamental nucleus of a healthy society. In this regard, we emphasize regular family worship, particularly at Sunday liturgy."[60] Notice that this statement grounds marriage and family in worship, not conventional political categories. The same is true of an earlier statement by America's Orthodox bishops that appeals to scripture, tradition, and the sacramental nature of the life-giving union of man and woman in the image of God.[61] The Church calls people ultimately to a life of holiness, not to a politicized agenda.

In contemporary American culture, Orthodoxy's official teachings on marriage, sexual ethics, abortion, and euthanasia stand in clear contrast with some sets of political opinion. Strands of Orthodox thought on capital punishment, environmental stewardship, the Israeli-Palestinian conflict, and the dangers of greed and consumerism, however, are at odds with other varieties of political thought. It should not be surprising that the Church's vision of God's intentions for the collective life of humanity is not identical with those of worldly interest groups that prize their own power above all else. Regardless of the matter at stake, Orthodoxy does not approach social ethics in light of popular western categories such as human rights, the pursuit of the greatest good for the greatest number, or philosophical commitments about liberty. Instead, the focus is on challenging by word and deed the lie that this world and its power arrangements are the fundamental truths of life; for in reality, the entire creation—including every social order—will find fulfillment and healing only by participating in the holiness of the Kingdom of God.[62]

The Orthodox Church does not tell its members how to vote in given elections, and there is not unanimity on what particular forms of political activism are most fitting or appropriate even on matters where there is a

---

60. Assembly of Canonical Orthodox Bishops of North and Central America, "Message to the Faithful."

61. Traketellis, et al., "Pan Orthodox Consensus on Same-Sex Unions."

62. Guroian, *Incarnate Love*, 134–35.

consensus on moral teaching. For example, some Orthodox enthusiastically support efforts to defeat candidates and referendums that would legalize same-sex unions of any kind. Their rationale is that Christian marriage is the fulfillment of the union of man and woman, who were created together in the image of God. To fail to advocate for a traditional view of marriage is to cooperate with society's rejection of deep truths about the human being and the family. By opposing such changes through the political process, they do what they can to preserve the unique role of marriage in society, and thus to bring the culture more fully in harmony with God's purposes for men and women. On the other hand, some Orthodox moralists are libertarians who think that regulating marriage and family is simply none of the government's business. Instead of devoting time and energy to the rancor of partisan politics, they ask for freedom for the Church—and everyone else in society—to handle questions of marriage and family as they see fit.[63]

Father Thomas Hopko provides a different perspective, as he affirms the rights of same-sex couples to civil unions and domestic partnerships with attendant legal and social benefits. He also insists that "Orthodox Christianity may never bless or countenance unions between persons of the same sex that contend to be *marriages* in the same sense as marriages between men and women." When it comes to the question of same-sex marriages recognized by civil law, he calls for believers to tolerate, but not to "approve or affirm them as acceptable to human being and life."[64]

Vigen Guroian finds it likely that civil unions and marriages between people of the same sex, as well as polygamous marriages, will eventually gain legal status throughout the US. He draws on the experience of Orthodox communities in Muslim-majority societies which "have lived and in some places continue to live under arrangements in which civil marriage and religious marriage are clearly distinguished in law and practice."[65] He suggests that the clergy not sign marriage certificates in states with same-sex marriage so as to separate society's parody of this union with the true sacramental union of man and woman. "By taking such action, the church would lodge its profound disagreement with the state's unilateral and theologically mistaken redefinition of marriage."[66] These regrettable circumstances, nonetheless, create an opportunity for the Church to affirm

63. See Engelhardt, *The Foundations of Christian Bioethics*, 395.
64. Hopko, *Christian Faith and Same-Sex Attraction*, 83–85.
65. Guroian, *Rallying the Really Human Things*, 122–23.
66. Ibid., 123–25.

the distinctiveness of Christian marriage in contrast to the declining mores of secular society. There is a clear consensus about the spiritual and moral standing of marriage within Eastern Christianity. There are, however, different views on how to bear witness to that consensus in the larger culture.

Of course, the fundamental matters at stake in society's stance on same-sex marriage go much deeper than the legal status available to homosexual couples. In a society that basically endorses sex for anyone who consents and has already trivialized matrimony, it is understandable that same-sex marriage appeals to many as a fairly mild way to provide recognition and stability to those who intend to bond permanently with a member of the same sex. There is a certain consistency to the argument that a society which sees no moral distinction between heterosexual and homosexual intimacy ought to recognize the marriages of gays and lesbians just as it does those of straight couples. In a culture with hardly any sense of chastity, to privilege any sexual relationship over another may well appear to be irrational and unfair.

Theologically, however, the issues are quite different, for human beings are created male and female in God's image. Our identity as a man or a woman is not spiritually insignificant, but a sign of who we are as unique persons. In light of Jesus Christ's full humanity with a physical body, it is clear that a life of holiness requires disciplining our sexual behavior in ways that sanctify our embodied human nature (1 Cor 6:12–20). No relationship other than that of male and female is capable of bringing new life into the world, which is surely at least a clue to God's intentions for both sexuality and the family. A society that no longer views the man-woman relationship as uniquely fundamental to our existence—biologically, socially, and spiritually—has turned away from a deep truth about what it means to be human.

The differences between male and female make the union of marriage life-giving, complementary, and a path to holiness. By the restoration of the primal unity of man and woman in God, Christian marriage becomes a sign of the salvation of all humanity and of the creation itself. The challenge is not only to say such words about marriage, but to live them out in ways that draw others to Christ and his Church. That remains the most fundamental political action of the Christian community: to embody a life that manifests the Lord's victory over death, that heals our broken, corrupt humanity—body and soul, male and female. Christians are called to embody the unique glory of marriage and family as a path to participation in the life of the Holy Trinity. Such an example will draw people to a life of holiness and provide living proof of the wisdom of the Church's constant teaching. Chastity is not a battle to be won or lost at the ballot box, but through the daily struggle to lead a holy life.

The cultures, forms of government, and economic systems in which Eastern Christians find themselves vary widely around the world. It is safe to say, however, that we are responsible for discerning how to witness to the social implications of God's Kingdom even as we live within earthly kingdoms where our options are inevitably limited. In American democracy, for example, voting for one candidate instead of another is rarely a choice for perfect good instead of perfect evil. At times, there may not be a candidate on the ballot for whom we can vote in good conscience. Nonetheless, believers should prayerfully discern how to live out the teachings of the faith in relation to the given set of circumstances in which they find themselves. Prudent judgment and a conscience formed by solid Christian teaching and practice are necessary to determine what candidates, parties, or ballot initiatives best serve God's purposes for the collective life of humanity. Christian citizens should vote accordingly. Politics remains, however, the art of the possible and faithful people with identical moral commitments may disagree, for example, over what specific candidates and policies will best serve to protect life in the womb, provide more appropriate care for the sick and dying, encourage the flourishing of families, and enact better stewardship of natural and economic resources.

In comparison with many Western churches, the Orthodoxy does not have a precisely defined political theology and rarely identifies itself with a partisan agenda in the American sense. At the risk of stretching the category too far, voting and other forms of political action may well involve us in what the Church calls involuntary sin. These are sins that we do not intend, may not even know about, and cannot reasonably avoid. For example, someone may in good conscience support a candidate or party whose positions do not line up perfectly with the social vision of Eastern Christianity. That candidate may enact policies that are contrary to God's purposes in various ways. But if voters did the best they could under the circumstances with limited options, the spiritual gravity is not nearly as great as that of voting for a candidate because he promised to increase abortion rates, start pointless wars, promote sexual immorality, and disregard orphans. Even a candidate whose positions fit perfectly with Christian values may exercise bad judgment, be overwhelmed by circumstances, or otherwise end up doing more harm than good. In the world as we know it, there are surely politicians who cynically use religious and moral rhetoric to gain votes without ever intending to act upon their promises. There is a brokenness, an imperfection, about the collective life of fallen humanity that is impossible to avoid completely in politics and social life. Perhaps that is part of the reason Orthodox pray for the forgiveness of "sins voluntary and involuntary, of word and of deed, of knowledge and of ignorance" before taking Communion. No matter how we vote or live, we stand in constant need of the Lord's mercy.

The Christian witness is certainly not simply or primarily a matter of voting, of course. The first calling of disciples is to be faithful to their Lord, which is a vocation fulfilled through the life of the Body of Christ, not by isolated individuals. Particular members are formed, strengthened, and encouraged to life faithfully each day as they offer themselves and the world for blessing and fulfillment in God. Such a path of discipleship grounded in the Church is necessary in order to speak with integrity about matters that extend bound the visible boundaries of the community of faith. For example, Christians—both individually and collectively—must pursue sexual purity throughout their lives and fidelity in marriage if they are to have any standing to participate in societal debates about the family or sexual ethics. Congregations and families have ample opportunity to live out the Christian witness on how to raise children, to welcome pregnant women in difficult circumstances, and to provide care to sick and lonely people. It is a small endeavor, but at St. Luke we sponsor a table each year at the fundraising dinner for Pregnancy Resources of Abilene, which is a wonderful ecumenical Christian ministry that provides pro-life health care and counseling to expectant mothers and the fathers of their children. The organization even has ministries to women who have had abortions and to the men who fathered aborted children.

If our own house is not in order, no one will take seriously our speeches, demonstrations, or activism on moral and social issues. We will not speak with integrity if we do not actually live out the moral and spiritual agenda that we teach in ways that cannot be confused with a merely worldly agenda. If believers become addicted to spending money in self-indulgent ways or without regard to the needs of the poor, rhetoric about caring for the needy and vulnerable will fall on deaf ears. If patterns of convenience lead us to abuse the abuse the environment because recycling and conserving energy are too difficult, the language of stewardship will amount to so many empty words. If we make our own economic interests the highest standard to the exclusion of concern for others or the common good, we will end up loving money more than we do our neighbors. True Christian faithfulness costs something and requires us to die to self as we grow into the life of the Kingdom. Equating the Christian witness with simply joining in the regular political fray by running our mouths or carrying signs is a sorry substitute for the difficult, long road of following in the costly way of Jesus Christ. It is also to place worldly power and domination before taking up the cross.

Whether as a result of constant media bombardment through the Internet, talk radio, or partisan cable news channels, many people on the right and the left—and the shrinking middle—seem to have succumbed to the dangerous temptation to think that the real playing field for matters of Christian faithfulness is located in mainstream politics. Eastern Christianity reminds us, however, that no earthly realm is the Kingdom of God or the Body of Christ. It is an illusion of Western democracy that you or I rule our nation, let alone the world. What we have real responsibility for is much smaller: our own souls and those with whom we share a common life in a substantive way. Of course, our lives are linked not only with members of our families and congregations, but also with fellow citizens of our nation and world, not to mention those of past and future generations. We must do the best we can to offer ourselves and our world to the Lord for the fulfillment of his purposes for us and the entire creation. How we vote or what bumper sticker we put on our car is a very small part of how we serve God, and even then there is not a one-to-one correspondence between any worldly political movement and the Holy Trinity.

Religious groups that are strongly identified with politics risk becoming so entangled in debates shaped by interest groups that their distinctive witness is obscured. To give the impression of being merely a political party at prayer is a good way to make people think that the church has little to say to the world that the world does not already know on its own terms. If all Christianity provides is a bit of spiritual inspiration to live, act, and think like dominant groups in our society already do, then we must ask seriously what it means to be salt and light. In addition, politics makes strange bedfellows and we must be careful not to tempt anyone to confuse the gospel of Jesus Christ with a partisan political movement. Parties are collections of interest groups and ideological advocates. There is a danger in aligning the Christian witness so closely with them that we give the impression that the faith unambiguously endorses a whole range of positions that may have nothing to do with Christianity or are even contrary to it. Those who disagree on some extraneous partisan issue may then think that they must also reject Jesus Christ.

Part of being salt and light is providing a distinctive witness, not blending into the background with everyone else. The cultural witness of the Church should not be reduced to questions of who we will support—like any other interest group—to be in charge of the government in order to serve our agendas. The fullness of the faith must not be reduced to passing laws or engaging in contemporary culture wars or partisanship, but instead calls for a spiritual vision and way of living that grows from worship, fasting, almsgiving, reconciliation, and the other disciplines of the Church. The most fundamental political action of the Christian community is not to support candidates or even the moral reform of society, but to become a living icon of God's Kingdom that draws others to the salvation of the world. Orthodoxy's most fundamental cultural engagement is neither American nor Russian, neither liberal nor conservative, neither Republican nor Democrat. It is to be faithful as the Body of Christ; everything else grows from that fundamental commitment and nothing can take its place.

Though we rarely think of worship as having any political or cultural significance, the Divine Liturgy grounds the Church's witness to God's salvation; indeed, it enacts the offering of our lives to the Lord that we should make every day as we enter more fully into the life of the Holy Trinity. Instead of living according to the standards of the kingdoms of this world, the Liturgy begins with proclamation of our ultimate destiny: "Blessed is the Kingdom of the Father, and of the Son, and of the Holy Spirit." Petitions follow immediately for "the peace from above and the salvation of our souls" and "for the peace of the whole world, the good estate of the holy churches of God, and the union of all men." Then there are more prayers for God's mercy upon the poor, sick, and needy, as well as for the governing authorities and armed forces.

The Church enters spiritually into the peace of the heavenly banquet in the Liturgy, into the Wedding Feast of the Lamb as described in the book of Revelation. We offer bread and wine as symbols of the whole creation for their and our fulfillment in the Kingdom. "Thine own of Thine own, we offer unto Thee in behalf of all and for all," the priest proclaims immediately before invoking the Holy Spirit to transform these gifts into the Body and Blood of Christ. The Church prays here for the salvation of the entire world through the redemptive work of the Lord. More prayers follow for God's blessing upon the Church, the sick, the suffering, and victims of justice, as well as for the armed forces that they will know "peaceful times that we, in their tranquility, may lead a calm and peaceful life in all reverence and godliness."

The Divine Liturgy is an enacted liturgical icon of our salvation. Through our participation in the life, death, and resurrection of Jesus Christ, we enter into heavenly peace and holiness. Not something reserved for the distant eschatological future, the blessings of sharing in the eternal life of God are already available to those who call upon the name of the Lord with faith, hope, and love. Even the most pleasant, peaceable, and just society is the not the fullness of the Kingdom and suffers from spiritual and moral corruption in many ways. Nonetheless, all goodness is the work of God and we should rejoice whenever any society does better rather than worse, whenever the Lord's purposes for humanity are fulfilled even imperfectly and partially. Christians should be the leaven in all societies, inspiring by word and deed anyone who will pay attention to the possibility of entering more fully into the blessedness for which we were created.

The salvation of human beings is an infinite journey of participating in the holiness of God. It is the dynamic process of *theosis* as we become partakers of the divine nature by ongoing repentance and growth in Christ. We are not isolated individuals, but persons in communion who flourish in relationship with one another. We cannot pretend that our relationship with the Lord is not shaped decisively by our relationships with other people, including how we treat others and organize our common life. The Kingdom of God is a social image of salvation that in many biblical passages concerns meeting fundamental human needs, overcoming divisions between people that are the result of sin, and reversing the order of the world as we know it. Of course, humanity cannot build the fullness of God's reign by its own power, but societies may be more or less in line with his intended purposes for social life. Surely, how any community organizes its common life reflects the spiritual state of its members and shapes them for better or worse.

God wants to heal, bless, and transform every dimension of the creation as part of a new heaven and a new earth. Nothing is intrinsically profane, evil, or beyond his concern. Hence, the political life of humanity is not evil in and of itself or necessarily cut off from holiness or salvation. Neither is it a way to usher in the fullness of God's reign by dint of our own efforts.

We are too weak and corrupt for that. But our social interactions are a way that we become more or less the kinds of people God created us to be in his image and likeness. The more the collective life of humanity provides a glimpse—no matter how faint—of the coming Kingdom, the better. The more the ways of the world come in line with the faithful witness of the Church, the more fully society serves God's purposes. Church and state are distinct institutions, but what people believe and how they live are not ultimately separate matters. The witness of the Church and its members should model the blessed and truly human existence to which Jesus Christ calls everyone in ways that challenge the corruptions of every social order. If Christians fail to respond faithfully to that most fundamental vocation, they will have nothing to contribute to the culture. But if we fulfill it even partially, then we will be salt and light in our words and our deeds by calling the world to holiness. The Orthodox Church invites its members, and ultimately everyone else, to enter into the life of the Kingdom.

CONCLUSION

A FINAL THOUGHT

IF NOTHING ELSE, I hope that this book has challenged you to think "outside the box" of the Christianity that you know. In other words, there are alternatives to the standard divisions of belief and practice that we are used to when it comes to religion in our culture. All of those divisions are much younger than the faith of the Orthodox Church, which understands itself to be the fullness of the Body of Christ born at Pentecost by the power of the Holy Spirit. To appreciate the insights of Eastern Christianity does not keep us from being Americans or people who live, think, and act according to the social realities of the twenty-first century. The good people of St. Luke look, dress, and behave pretty much like their mostly Protestant neighbors. Those who encounter this ancient faith will, however, find challenge and enrichment for their lives as they learn to bow before the great "I AM" Who is beyond even the best rational definition of any time and place.

If you would like to learn more about Eastern Orthodoxy, the nearest Orthodox parish will probably be more helpful than the nearest library. As I hope that the preceding chapters made clear, we do not know God through collections of abstract ideas found in books, but through an encounter with the Body of Christ empowered by the Holy Spirit. Yes, that means the Church as manifest in any Orthodox parish and the people who worship there. Check out their service schedule and show up when you can, especially for the usual Saturday evening service of Great Vespers. By Orthodox standards, this is a fairly simple and brief service of evening prayer, usually without a sermon. Service books may be available, but the best approach is simply to let the chant, incense, and readings wash over you as you open your heart to God in prayer. In the average congregation, attendance at Saturday vespers is not large; it is unusual in our culture for people to attend church services of any variety on both Saturday night and

Sunday morning. Take advantage of the relatively low attendance to focus on the Lord, not on feeling out of place. Especially if it is your first time in an Orthodox service, just do your best to pray. Trust me, the priest will simply be glad that you are there and will be happy to answer your questions. At St. Luke, we have had fairly regular visitors at vespers who have other commitments on Sunday morning. Everyone is welcome to pray with us whenever they can. No strings attached.

Also consider getting an Orthodox prayer book and using it as best you can to open your heart to God. There is really nothing as spiritually beneficial as regular prayer from the depths our being. Memorize the Jesus Prayer—"Lord Jesus Christ, Son of God, have mercy on me a sinner"—and pray it quietly and meditatively whenever you have a chance. Devote time each day to reading the Psalms, the four gospels, and the rest of the Bible. As your health and life circumstances allow, practice a light form of fasting or self-denial. There are very few who will not profit spiritually from learning to say no to some of their self-centered desires, even in small ways. If you would like guidance in how to embrace these practices, ask the priest or any experienced Orthodox believer.

It is good to read books about Orthodoxy, but actually participating—even if only a little bit—in the worship, prayer, and spiritual disciplines of the Church is the best way to benefit from the distinctive insights and practices of Eastern Christianity. God is not a rational concept and theology is not intellectual speculation. We know God by the experience of sharing in His life, and anyone with an open mind and heart will find spiritual sustenance by participating as best they can in the spiritual life of the Church.

Of course, I am glad that you read this book, but let that be only the beginning of your encounter with the fullness of Orthodox Christianity, not the end. Do your best to bow before the Holy Mystery of the Father, the Son, and Holy Spirit. Even though it will complicate your spiritual life and there is no telling where the journey will lead, you will be glad you did.

BIBLIOGRAPHY

Alfeyev, Hilarion. *The Mystery of Faith: An Introduction to the Teaching and Spirituality of the Orthodox Church.* London: Darton, Longman, and Todd, 2002.
Assembly of Canonical Orthodox Bishops of North and Central America. "Message to the Faithful." 2012. No Pages. Online: http://oca.org/news/headline-news/assembly-of-bishops-concludes-three-day-meeting-issues-statement-to-all-fai.
Athanasius. *The Life of Antony and The Letter to Marcellinus.* Mahwah, NJ: Paulist, 1980.
Bartholomew I. *Encountering the Mystery: Understanding Orthodox Christianity Today.* New York: Doubleday, 2008.
———. *In the World, Yet Not of the World.* Edited by Father John Chryssavgis. New York: Fordham University Press, 2010.
Basil the Great. *On the Holy Spirit.* Yonkers, NY: St. Vladimir's Seminary Press, 2011.
Behr-Sigel, Elisabeth. *The Ministry of Women in the Church.* Redondo Beach, CA: Oakwood, 1991.
Belonick, Deborah Malacky. *Feminism in Christianity: An Orthodox Christian Response.* Yonkers, NY: St. Vladimir's Seminary Press, 2012.
Berry, Wendell. *Sex, Economy, Freedom and Community.* New York: Pantheon, 1993.
Breck, John. *The Sacred Gift of Life: Orthodox Christianity and Bioethics.* Crestwood, NY: St. Vladimir's Seminary Press, 2000
Brownworth, Lars. *Lost to the West: The Forgotten Byzantine Empire that Rescued Western Civilization.* New York: Three Rivers, 2009.
Chryssavgis, John, ed. *Cosmic Grace, Humble Prayer: The Ecological Vision of the Green Patriarch Bartholomew I.* Grand Rapids: Eerdmans, 2003.
Chryssavgis, John. *In the Heart of the Desert: The Spirituality of the Desert Fathers and Mothers.* Bloomington, IN: World Wisdom, 2003.
Coniaris, Anthony M. *Making God Real in the Orthodox Home.* Minneapolis: Light and Life, 1977.
Douthat, Ross. *Bad Religion: How We Became a Nation of Heretics.* New York: Free Press 2012.
Engelhardt, H. Tristram, Jr. *The Foundations of Christian Bioethics.* Lisse: Swets & Zeitlinger, 2000.
Dreher, Rod. "Eastern Right: Conservative Minds Convert to Orthodox Christianity." *The American Conservative* (June 4, 2012). No Pages. Online: http://www.theamerican Conservative.com/articles/eastern-right-2.
Farley, Lawrence R. *Feminism and Tradition: Quiet Reflections on Ordination and Communion.* Yonkers, NY: St. Vladimir's Seminary Press, 2012.

———. *Let Us Attend: A Journey Through the Orthodox Divine Liturgy.* Ben Lomond, CA: Conciliar, 2007.

FitzGerald, Kyriaki Karidoyanes, ed. *Encountering Women of Faith: The St. Catherine's Vision Collection* 1. Berkeley, CA: InterOrthodox, 2005.

Gabriel, George S. *Mary: The Untrodden Portal of God.* Ridgewood, NJ: Zephyr, 2000.

Gagnon, Robert A. J. *The Bible and Homosexual Practice: Texts and Hermeneutics* Nashville: Abingdon, 2001.

Guroian, Vigen. *Incarnate Love: Essays in Orthodox Ethics.* Notre Dame, IN: University of Notre Dame Press, 1987

———. *Rallying the Really Human Things.* Wilmington, DE: ISI, 2005.

Hackel, Sergei. *Pearl of Great Price: The Life of Mother Maria Skobtsova 1891–1945.* Crestwood, NY: St. Vladimir's Seminary Press, 1982.

Harakas, Stanley. *Let Mercy Abound.* Brookline, MA: Holy Cross Orthodox, 1983.

———. *Living the Faith: The Praxis of Eastern Orthodox Ethics.* Minneapolis: Life and Life, 1992.

Hart, David Bentley. *Atheist Delusions: The Christian Revolution and Its Fashionable Enemies.* New Haven: Yale University Press, 2009.

Helgeland, R. J. Daly, et al. *Christians and the Military: The Early Experience.* Philadelphia: Fortress, 1985.

Herfurth, Kenneth L. "The *Theotokos*." BA honors diss., McMurry University, 2005.

Hopko, Thomas. *Christian Faith and Same-Sex Attraction: Eastern Orthodox Reflections.* Ben Lomond, CA: Conciliar, 2006.

Hopko, Thomas, ed. *Women and the Priesthood.* Crestwood, NY: St. Vladimir's Seminary Press, 1999.

John of Damascus. *Three Treatises on the Divine Images.* Crestwood, NY: St. Vladimir's Seminary Press, 2003.

Kelly, J. N. D. *Early Christian Doctrines.* San Francisco: HarperSanFrancisco, 1978.

Khoury, Maria. "Taybeh's Plea for the Last Christians of the Holy Land." *Road to Emmaus* 43 (Fall 2010) 3–43. Online: http://www.farahfoundation.org/UpdateZine.pdf.

Krueger, Derek. *Symeon the Holy Fool: Leontius's Life and the Late Antique City.* Berkeley: University of California Press, 1996.

Larchet, Jean-Claude. *Mental Disorders and Spiritual Healing: Teachings from the Early Christian East.* Hillsdale, NY: Angelico Press/Sophia Perennis, 2005.

Leithart, Peter J. *Defending Constantine: The Twilight of an Empire and the Dawn of Christendom.* Downers Grove, IL: InterVarsity, 2010.

LeMasters, "A Dynamic Praxis of Peace: Orthodox Social Ethics and Just Peacemaking." *Revista Teologica* 4 (2010) 69–82.

———. *The Goodness of God's Creation: How to Live as an Orthodox Christian/A Guide to Orthodox Ethics.* Salisbury, MA: Regina Orthodox, 2008.

———. *The Import of Eschatology in John Howard Yoder's Critique of "Constantinianism."* San Francisco: Mellen Research University Press, 1992

———. "Orthodox Perspectives on Peace, War and Violence." *The Ecumenical Review* 63.1 (March 2011) 54–61.

———. *Toward a Eucharistic Vision of Church, Family, Marriage, and Sex.* Minneapolis: Light and Life, 2004.

Limouris, Gennadios, ed. *The Place of the Woman in the Orthodox Church and the Question of the Ordination of Women.* Katerini, Greece: Tertios, 1992.

Lossky, Vladimir. *Orthodox Theology: An Introduction.* Crestwood, NY: St. Vladimir's Seminary Press, 1989.

"The Manhattan Declaration: A Call of Christian Conscience." November 20, 2009. No Pages. Online: http://www.firstthings.com/onthesquare/2009/11/manhattan-declaration58-a-call-of-christian-conscience.

Mathewes-Green, Frederica. *Gender: Men, Women, Sex, Feminism.* Ben Lomond, CA: Conciliar, 2002.

———. *The Jesus Prayer: The Ancient Desert Prayer that Tunes the Heart to God.* Brewster, MA: Paraclete, 2009.

———. *The Lost Gospel of Mary: The Mother of Jesus in Three Ancient Texts.* Brewster, MA: Paraclete, 2007.

———. "Women's Ordination." No pages. Online: http://www.frederica.com/writings/womens-ordination.html.

"Medieval Sourcebook: The Life of our Holy Mother Mary of Egypt." No pages. Online: http://www.fordham.edu/halsall/basis/maryegypt.asp.

McGuckin, John. *The Ascent of Christian Law: Patristic and Byzantine Formulations of a New Civilization.* Yonkers, NY: St. Vladimir's Seminary Press, 2012

Miller, Timothy S. "Orphanages and Philanthropy in Byzantium." *Road to Emmaus* 49 (Winter 2012) 53–78.

"A Moment of Truth: A Word of Faith, Hope, and Love from the Heart of Palestinian Suffering." Online: http://www.kairospalestine.ps/sites/default/Documents/English.pdf.

"National Religious Campaign Against Torture." No Pages. Online: http://www.nrcat.org/index.php?option=com_content&task=view&id=17&Itemid=46.

Noll, Mark. *The Scandal of the Evangelical Mind.* Grand Rapids: Eerdmans, 1994.

———. *Turning Points: Decisive Moments in the History of Christianity.* Grand Rapids: Baker Academic, 2000.

"An Orthodox View of Abortion: The *Amicus Curiae* Submitted to the Supreme Court." No Pages. Online: http://orthodoxinfo.com/praxis/abortion.aspx.

"Orthodoxy and Capital Punishment." No Pages. Online: http://www.incommunion.org/2008/02/24/orthodoxy-and-capital-punishment.

"Orthodoxy and the Environment." No Pages. Online: http://www.patriarchate.org/environment.

Palamas, Gregory. *The Triads.* Mahway, NJ: Paulist, 1983.

Palmer, G. E. H., et al. *The Philokalia* 1. London: Faber and Faber, 1979.

Papadakis, Aristeides, and John Meyendorff. *The Christian East and the Rise of the Papacy.* Crestwood, NY: St. Vladimir's Seminary Press, 1994

Pelikan, Jaroslav. *The Christian Tradition: A History of the Development of Doctrine, Vol. 2: The Spirit of Eastern Christendom (600-1700).* Chicago: University of Chicago Press, 1974.

"A Plea for Peace from the Orthodox Peace Fellowship of North America." No Pages. Online: http://www. www.incommunion.org/2004/10/19/iraq-apeal.

A Pocket Prayer Book for Orthodox Christians. Englewood, NY: Antiochian Orthodox Christian Archdiocese of North America, 1956.

"Record of Protest Against the Infringement of Religious Liberty by the Department of Health and Human Services." No Pages. Online: http://www.assemblyofbishops.org/news/2012protest-against-hhs."

Roberts, Alexander, and James Donaldson, eds. *Ante-Nicene Fathers*. Peabody, MA: Hendrickson, 1994.

Sakharov, Sophrony. *Saint Silouan the Athonite*. Essex: Stavropegic Monastery of St. John the Baptist, 1991.

Saliba, Philip. "On Iraq: Statement Issued by Metropolitan Philip." No Pages. Online: http://www.incommunion.org /2004/10/21/iraq-war-peace-appeals.

Schroeder, C. Paul. *On Social Justice: St. Basil the Great*. Crestwood, NY: St. Vladimir's Seminary Press, 2009

Sparks, Jack N., ed. *The Apostolic Fathers*. Minneapolis: Life and Life, 1978.

"Stepping into the Stream: An Interview with Alice C. Linsley." *The Road to Emmaus* 40 (Winter 2010) 3–37. Online: http://www.roadtoemmaus.net/back_issue_articles/ RTE /40Stepping_Into_The Stream.pdf.

Theodore the Studite. *On the Holy Icons*. Crestwood, NY: St. Vladimir's Seminary Press, 2001.

Theokritoff, Elizabeth. *Living in God's Creation: Orthodox Perspectives on Ecology*. Crestwood, NY: St. Vladimir's Seminary Press, 2009.

Theophan the Recluse. *The Spiritual Life: How To Be Attuned To It*. Platina, CA: St. Herman of Alaska Brotherhood, 2000.

Tkacz, Catherine Brown. "Women and the Church in the New Millennium." *St. Vladimir's Theological Quarterly* 52 (2008) 243–74.

Trakatellis, Demetrius, et al. "Pan Orthodox Consensus on Same-Sex Unions." No Pages. Online: http:// www.goarch.org/archdiocese/departments/marriage/interfaith/ guest-writers/ same-sex.

Ward, Benedicta. *The Lives of the Desert Fathers*. Kalamazoo, MI: Cistercian, 1980.

———. *The Sayings of the Desert Fathers*. Kalamazoo, MI: Cistercian, 1975.

Ware, Timothy (Kallistos). *The Inner Kingdom: Volume 1 of the Collected Works*. Crestwood, NY: St. Vladimir's Seminary Press, 2000.

———. *The Orthodox Church*. London: Penguin, 1997.

———. *The Orthodox Way*. Crestwood, NY: St. Vladimir's Seminary Press, 1999.

Webber, Meletios. *Bread and Water, Wine and Oil: An Orthodox Christian Experience of God*. Ben Lomond, CA: Conciliar, 2007.

Webster, Alexander F. C. *The Pacifist Option: The Moral Argument Against War in Eastern Orthodox Theology*. San Francisco: International Scholars Publications, 1998.

———. *The Price of Prophecy: Orthodox Churches on Peace, Freedom, and Security*. Grand Rapids: Eerdmans, 1995.

Webster, Alexander F. C., and Darrell Cole. *The Virtue of War: Reclaiming the Classic Christian Traditions East and West*. Salisbury, MA: Regina Orthodox, 2004.

Wesley, John. "A Letter to a Roman Catholic." No pages. Online: http://hitch.south.cx/ john-Wesleys-letter-to-a-roman-catholic.htm.

Williams, Benjamin, and Harold Anstall. *Orthodox Worship: A Living Continuity with the Synagogue, the Temple and the Early Church*. Minneapolis: Light and Life, 1990.

Winner, Lauren. *Real Sex: The Naked Truth About Chastity*. Grand Rapids: Brazos, 2005.

Wybrew, Hugh. *The Orthodox Liturgy: The Development of the Eucharistic Liturgy in the Byzantine Rite*. Crestwood, NY: St. Vladimir's Seminary Press, 1990.

Yannaras, Christos. *The Freedom of Morality*. Crestwood, NY: St. Vladimir's Seminary Press, 1984.

www.ingramcontent.com/pod-product-compliance
Lightning Source LLC
Chambersburg PA
CBHW022121160426
43197CB00009B/1105